Praise for
STAND FIRM AND ACT LIKE MEN

"We live in a time when there is nothing but confusion about what it means to be a man. Joby in his new book *Stand Firm and Act Like Men* answers this question with biblical clarity, conviction, and gospel-centered courage. This is not another cultural ideal—it is a reclamation of biblical manhood that leads with humility, strength, and love. It's timely, bold, and desperately needed."

—Dr. Mac Brunson, pastor of Valleydale Church

"*Dazed and Confused* was the name of a 1993 coming-of-age comedic film, but it also describes too many believers today regarding biblical manhood. God's Word is the answer when confusion reigns, and my friend Joby Martin offers sage biblical wisdom for men (and women) in this book. Grounded in Scripture and aware of the extremes of our day (like overly passive/overly aggressive), Joby roots the strength of manhood in the gospel and the pursuit of being increasingly like Jesus. The clarity needed in a confused world can be found here." —Ed Stetzer, dean, Talbot School of Theology

"Culture can't decide what it wants from men. The same society that can't even define what a woman is has the audacity to call masculinity 'toxic' one minute and then complain that men aren't stepping up the next. Meanwhile, much of the modern church has told men—implicitly or explicitly—that to be a 'good Christian,' they need to act more like women. The result? Countless men who are disciplined, responsible, and willing to lead are left wondering what a man even is—and how to become one. In *Stand Firm and Act Like Men*, Joby cuts through the noise. He doesn't rely on cultural fads, macho stereotypes, or 'red pill' ideology. Instead, he takes us straight to the Word of God. This book is a clear, unapologetic, and biblical vision of manhood. And here's the truth: You can't become what you don't understand. Joby helps men understand—truly and deeply—what God designed them to be."

—Kyle Thompson, founder, Undaunted.Life,
and host, *The Daily Blade*

"I've been in ministry since 1987 and I can't remember a time when the church and our nation needed tough and tender men of God more than right now. Thank God for this book! Joby writes like he preaches: with compassion, conviction, and clarity. He embodies the message of this book in his everyday life as a man who stands firm on the gospel and the Word of God. As 'masculinity' has been distorted, weaponized, and attacked in this generation, I pray that God will use *Stand Firm and Act Like Men* to renew a rich theology of manhood and revive a passion in the hearts of men to love, lead, and serve their families, the church, our nation, and the Lord Jesus Christ."

—Dr. Clayton King, evangelist, teaching pastor,
Biltmore Church and Newspring Church, and
author of *Reborn*, *Stronger*, and *Overcome*

"I grew up in church. I have been married for over twenty-five years. I am the proud dad of four kids. It's tempting to act like I have things figured out, but thankfully this book cuts right through that and reminds me what it truly means to be a man. Joby is funny, practical, and biblical."

—Brian Mosley, president of RightNow Media

"If you're a guy like me, trying to figure out how to follow Jesus, lead your family well, and not get lost in what the world says a man's supposed to be, this book is exactly what you need. Joby Martin has been one of the biggest influences in my life when it comes to understanding what real, godly manhood looks like. He doesn't sugarcoat anything. He shoots it straight, backs it with the Bible, and points everything back to Jesus. That's what you'll get in *Stand Firm and Act Like Men*, a solid, no-fluff guide to stepping up as the man God's called you to be. This book will challenge you, encourage you, and probably kick you in the teeth a little, but in the best kind of way. It'll make you look in the mirror, lay down your pride, and finally man up enough to admit that Jesus, not your talent, toughness, or titles, is what your family and your future really need. If you're serious about leading strong and leaving a legacy worth following, do yourself a favor and read this. I can guarantee you if we as men will read this book, take it to heart, and chase after Jesus with everything in us, we can change the world one legacy at a time!"

—Drew Parker, country music singer and songwriter

"My friend Joby Martin is one of the great Kingdom leaders of our generation. He is also one of the greatest men I know, not because he leads one of the largest and fastest-growing churches in America or because he is an accomplished author with many accolades. He is one of the greatest men I know because of who he is. Joby is a real man—a man of integrity, tenacity, and humility. He is a man of honor. I can think of no one more qualified to write this much-needed book. The fabric of civilization is families; as the fathers go, so goes the family. While society sees men as a problem, God sees men as the solution. We need a revival of biblical masculinity in America. This book has the power to spark that revival in men, and it's one that every man should read."

—Phil Hopper, author and lead pastor of Abundant Life Church

"This book is one page after another of motivational wisdom. It reminds me of a creed that my spiritual grandfather displayed into his eighties when his body was winding down after a hard-fought life: 'This life ain't about playing it safe or staying clean. It's about charging hard, getting scarred up for the Kingdom, and sliding into heaven worn out, mud on your face, blood on your knuckles, and fire in your bones—shouting, "Holy s**t, Lord—what a ride!"' My friend Joby has written a book that calls out the best in me and other men. We all need it!"

—Brian Tome, founder of Crossroads Church and Mancamp

"I am so thankful for Joby Martin's new book *Stand Firm and Act Like Men*! With his characteristic loving directness, engaging humor, personal illustrations, and theological precision, Joby calls us up to biblical manhood. This is a book you will not only want to read and re-read, but one you will want to get into the hands of the men around you. I know I will!"

—Dr. Bruce Frank, lead pastor of Biltmore Church in western North Carolina and speaker on the radio program *The Vertical Life*

"Once again, Joby Martin has hit the mark. In a world where genuine biblical manhood has been obscured by goofy narcissistic definitions by some and canceled as toxic by others, Joby clears out the fog and points to reality that for too long has been hidden in plain sight."

—Larry Osborne, author and pastor of North Coast Church, California

"Joby's new book is truly a gift to us guys, and the potential impact reaches our spouse, kids, friends, and co-workers as well. It's filled with wit and wisdom, providing an honest, clear, and biblical picture of what true manhood looks like. *Stand Firm and Act Like Men* is an enjoyable read that packs a punch. A needed punch that is challenging and yet encouraging. Job's new book offers a Kingdom perspective in a practical manner. You will love this book!"

—Dan Reiland, author, leadership coach, husband, dad, and grandfather

"In a world quick to declare masculinity in crisis, Pastor Joby Martin offers a powerful, biblically grounded antidote. *Stand Firm and Act Like Men* cuts through the confusion, revealing that true manhood isn't about cultural stereotypes, but about surrendering to God, leading with love, and standing firm in faith. Through a clear and compelling walk through 1 Corinthians 16:13, he guides readers to understand who men are called to be, how they should act, and what it truly means to live as a man of God in today's complex world. This book is an essential guide for any man seeking to understand and embody the strength, purpose, and calling God intends."

—Léonce B. Crump Jr., author of *Renovate* and *The Resilience Factor*, and founder of United Church

"Joby Martin is a passionate pastor and compelling communicator who challenges men to think deeply, live boldly, and follow Jesus with courage. His voice is needed, and his heart for men as well as the next generation is clear in these pages."

—Doug Fields, pastor, author, and cofounder of Download Youth Ministry

STAND FIRM & ACT LIKE MEN

Becoming the Man You Were Created to Be
Instead of Who the World Says You Are

JOBY MARTIN
with CHARLES MARTIN

New York Nashville

Copyright © 2025 by Joseph P. Martin III
Foreword copyright © 2025 by Matt Carter

Cover design by Darren Welch. Cover copyright © 2025 by Hachette Book Group, Inc.

Hachette Book Group supports the right to free expression and the value of copyright. The purpose of copyright is to encourage writers and artists to produce the creative works that enrich our culture.

The scanning, uploading, and distribution of this book without permission is a theft of the author's intellectual property. If you would like permission to use material from the book (other than for review purposes), please contact permissions@hbgusa.com. Thank you for your support of the author's rights.

FaithWords
Hachette Book Group
1290 Avenue of the Americas, New York, NY 10104
Faithwords.com
@Faithwords / @FaithWordsBooks

First Edition: October 2025

FaithWords is a division of Hachette Book Group, Inc. The FaithWords name and logo are trademarks of Hachette Book Group, Inc.

The publisher is not responsible for websites (or their content) that are not owned by the publisher.

The Hachette Speakers Bureau provides a wide range of authors for speaking events. To find out more, go to hachettespeakersbureau.com or email HachetteSpeakers@hbgusa.com.

FaithWords books may be purchased in bulk for business, educational, or promotional use. For information, please contact your local bookseller or the Hachette Book Group Special Markets Department at special.markets@hbgusa.com.

All Scripture quotations, unless otherwise indicated, are taken from The ESV® Bible (The Holy Bible, English Standard Version®), © 2001 by Crossway, a publishing ministry of Good News Publishers. Used by permission. All rights reserved.

Scripture quotations marked (NIV) are taken from the Holy Bible, New International Version®, NIV®. Copyright © 1973, 1978, 1984, 2011 by Biblica, Inc.™ Used by permission of Zondervan. All rights reserved worldwide. www.zondervan.com. The "NIV" and "New International Version" are trademarks registered in the United States Patent and Trademark Office by Biblica, Inc.™

Scripture quotations marked (NKJV) are taken from the New King James Version®. Copyright © 1982 by Thomas Nelson. Used by permission. All rights reserved.

Print book interior design by Marie Mundaca

Library of Congress Cataloging-in-Publication Data

Names: Martin, Joby author | Martin, Charles, 1969- author
Title: Stand firm and act like men : becoming the man you were created to be instead of who the world says you are / Joby Martin with Charles Martin.
Description: First edition. | New York ; Nashville : Faith Words, 2025.
Identifiers: LCCN 2025020057 | ISBN 9781546008217 hardcover | ISBN 9781546008231 ebook
Subjects: LCSH: Masculinity—Religious aspects—Christianity | Christian men—Religious life
Classification: LCC BV4528.2 .M3239 2025 | DDC 248.8/42—dc23/eng/20250707
LC record available at https://lccn.loc.gov/2025020057

ISBN: 978-1-5460-0821-7 (hardcover), 978-1-5460-0823-1 (ebook)

Printed in the United States of America

LSC-C

Printing 7, 2026

I dedicate this to the men that have shown me how to stand firm and act like a man. Thank you Daddy, Lars, Bill, Coach Bull, and Jerry.

Be watchful,
stand firm *in the faith,*
act like men,
be strong.
Let all that you do be done in love.

1 Corinthians 16:13–14

Therefore take up the whole armor
   of God,
that you may be able to **withstand** *in*
   the evil day,
and having done all,
to **stand firm**.
Stand therefore,
having fastened on the belt of truth,
and having put on the breastplate of
   righteousness.

Ephesians 6:13–14

CONTENTS

A Note on the Text — xv

Foreword — xvii

INTRODUCTION: Where Have All the Good Men Gone? — 1

CHAPTER 1: What Is a Man? — 23

CHAPTER 2: Be Watchful — 53

CHAPTER 3: Stand Firm — 87

CHAPTER 4: Be Strong — 121

CHAPTER 5: Love Is… — 149

CHAPTER 6: Are You Ready to Stand Firm and Act Like a Man? — 173

Final Thoughts — 191

Acknowledgments — *201*

A NOTE ON THE TEXT

Almost all direct scripture quotes in this book come from the English Standard Version. In some cases, I've simply paraphrased instead of quoting directly from a published translation; these passages are set in italics.

FOREWORD

As I write these words, I've recently crossed into my fifty-first year of living on this planet. Throughout those years, I've become increasingly convinced that the lack of genuine biblical manhood is *the root* of the overwhelming majority of society's problems. I hope you didn't breeze past that word: *biblical*. Because the root issue of our problems is not a lack of *manhood*, but a lack of *biblical manhood*. And the distinction between the two is deeper and wider than the distinction between Pastor Joby Martin and a Satanist, anti-hunting activist from the Pacific Northwest.

You see, regardless of your religion, race, ethnicity, gender, socio-economic status, or political affiliation, there's one reality that all of us can agree on: The world is messed up. It's broken, and it's in desperate need of healing. Our problem is that we tend to point the finger at other groups and argue that if they would get their act together the world would be a better place. But all throughout Scripture, when God was looking to intervene and bring healing to a society, He only looked one place...His People.

FOREWORD

If my people who are called by my name, will humble themselves and pray and seek my face and turn from their wicked ways, then I will hear from heaven, and I will forgive their sin and will heal their land.

2 Chronicles 7:14 (NIV)

But let's take it one step further. As God turns His eyes to us, those who are called by His name, we can make a pretty strong argument that first and foremost, He's looking to His men to stand firm and be the leader, lover, and warrior He's called us to be. Think about it: When Adam and Eve sinned, it was Eve who took the first bite and handed the fruit to her husband. But when the two of them were hiding from God, naked and ashamed in their sin, who did God call out to in order to hold them accountable? It wasn't Eve. It was Adam. The man. Today is no different. In the brokenness and dysfunction that is our world, men, God's eyes are squarely on us.

While this fantastic book is ultimately for everyone, men, I want to offer a challenge to you. Don't pick up this book, maybe glance over it, then go on with life as usual. Pick it up and devour it. Don't start it, finish it. Dig deeply and be transformed by the truths Pastor Joby teaches in these well-written pages. Make no mistake, the world is broken, but our God is bigger and more powerful than all of it. So let's step boldly and confidently into our noble calling to *Stand Firm and Act Like Men*!

Matt Carter
—Pastor and author of *The Real Win*
with Colt McCoy

STAND FIRM & ACT LIKE MEN

Introduction

WHERE HAVE ALL THE GOOD MEN GONE?

So there I was.
It was 1992ish. Spring semester of my freshman year at Virginia Commonwealth University. I had joined a fraternity, and my brothers were going to spend spring break in places that I couldn't afford, so I just decided to go visit my mom in Columbia, South Carolina, and brought my buddy, Aaron.

We were both eighteen years old, dumb as sticks, and buff as linebackers 'cause all we did was work out. Eight-pack abs, no body fat—we thought we were the jam.

We got to Mom's house, and pretty quick we realized we were bored, so we decided it'd be a good idea to go on a canoe trip on the Saluda River. I don't know why we thought this would be a good idea, as neither one of us had ever been on a canoe trip. I'd spent some time fishing with my dad in a jon boat, but never a canoe. And, looking back, it never really occurred to me that the motor on the back of my dad's fishing boat was the thing that solved all the problems we were about to encounter. But again, we were eighteen.

So we rented a canoe, which involved having to put down a $100 deposit. That was most of the money we possessed at the time. We tied the canoe to the top of my Chevrolet S10 pickup, which was made all the more manly by the bumper sticker that read, IT'S NOT THE CAR YOU DRIVE BUT THE SIZE OF THE ARM HANGING OUT THE WINDOW THAT MATTERS. What can I say? You can't hide money. We looked like Sanford and Son pulling up to the ramp, but we didn't care. You couldn't stop us.

Now, normally for a canoe trip you'd need two vehicles: one at the drop-off spot and one at the pickup spot. But we didn't have two vehicles, and we didn't have time to be bothered with the details. Just let us in the water. Have you seen these pecs? We can handle whatever this river throws at us. We're tough as nails.

We reasoned that we would either paddle our way upstream as far as we could, then just turn and float back. Or we would float down, then beach the canoe and just tote it back up the bank. Either way, it was no problem. We knew enough to know that we'd need some food, so we filled a cooler, loaded it into the canoe, launched, and started paddling. No sooner had we started paddling than we kicked off our flip-flops and took our shirts off because, I mean, have you seen these arms? They didn't just happen. Sun's out, guns out.

And, by God's grace—because as you can tell I wasn't all that smart—I tied the keys to my S10 inside my Umbro shorts. When we got in the river, we immediately realized we wouldn't be paddling upstream. No can do. It didn't look like much current, but the water flow was deceiving. It was a lot of current and it was moving. Which should have told us something, but don't bother us with the details. We got this. Realizing we weren't paddling upriver, we turned and began paddling downstream.

And life was great for about five minutes.

As the distance clicked by, we reasoned that when we'd been far enough—and we didn't really specify how far that was—we'd turn toward the bank, beach the canoe, and just tote it back upstream. In reality, our decision-making was this—let's do easy things first and we'll deal with the fallout later. So, we started the float down and life was good. It was beautiful. There weren't too many people. We had this.

Somewhere downriver—and I can't remember if it was one mile or ten, but in my memory it seemed like we were in a different county—we got to the point where we started asking, *How are we going to get back to the truck?* It seemed like a mature time and place to start asking that. Realizing we might have floated down a bit far, I sunk the paddle into the rear of the canoe, like a rudder, and turned us toward shore. Aaron was paddling, and we were now perpendicular to the current, which wouldn't normally have been a problem, except that it pushed us against a log at the surface of the water, which was also perpendicular. The river pressed us against the downed tree, and within about half a millisecond the pressure of the current stopped any forward progress. Water started pouring in over the gunnels—the sides of the canoe. Then in about another half a millisecond, the current sucked the entire canoe under the log.

When we surfaced, the canoe, the cooler, the paddles, our clothes—everything we had brought save our Umbros and one set of car keys—were floating downriver. Lost. We swam to the shore and stood on the bank watching our life disappear around the next bend. With no other option, we started bushwhacking through the swamp back upriver. We weren't really in danger of dying, but we'd lost pretty much everything we owned, not to mention the fact that we could kiss our deposit goodbye. This was not good. If I was going to be this stupid, I should've gone to the beach with my brothers.

As we walked through the swamp barefoot, skirting snakes and sharp things, I could hear the echo of my daddy, who told me a hundred times that the only thing you can do in flip-flops is get your butt kicked (although he didn't use those words). The second thing I was seeing in my mind's eye was John McClane walking across those shards of glass in that office in the Nakitomi Tower in bare feet. Meanwhile, my flip-flops were floating toward the ocean.

We were a couple miles from where we needed to be, so we started making our way back upriver, which was a slow process because sometimes we were in the water pulling ourselves upstream using branches, and the rest of the time we were tiptoeing through a swamp filled with anacondas. And honestly, it was kind of quiet between me and Aaron right then. We both knew we were idiots, but we weren't quite at the point where we wanted to confess that to the other. After about ten quiet minutes, we heard a boat motor, and it sounded like it was getting closer. Coming upriver. A minute later, this ski boat thing—one of those boats with a windshield and the driver sitting on the right side—came winding its way upriver.

And, to our great surprise, it was towing our canoe. What's more, inside the canoe was our cooler and a couple of paddles. Unfortunately, we never saw our flip-flops again, but who's complaining? We flagged the guy down and he told us they were tubing downriver when all this stuff started floating by them. Looked like somebody'd had a yard sale. So they policed all the stuff and honestly, they said they thought we had died and they were hauling this stuff back upriver for the authorities to have as evidence. No kidding, they thought we'd drowned. Not only did they return all our stuff, not to mention our dignity, but they towed us back to the ramp and my truck.

Despite our stupidity, God sent an older man with the right equipment and experience that day, and he saved us and all our stuff. We even got our deposit back. That guy literally saved us.

I hope and pray that's what this book does for you.

The Bible is very clear about what it means to stand up and act like men, and what it takes for a man to become a man. Bottom line: Manhood is bestowed. It is passed down. From man to boy. (Mommas, if you're reading this, hold on. I have some good news to say to you. Just hang in there and keep reading.)

The fact is many of us boys have flipped our own canoes, and our lives are floating downriver. To make matters worse, we have bought into the lie that other boys can help us reach manhood. That boys can make men. It doesn't work that way. Not in the Bible. Not in real life. My prayer for you is that through the power of the Holy Spirit, the Word of God, and maybe a little of my own experience, this book might lead you on a path to biblical manhood.

Sometimes in my church, single women ask me, "Pastor, where have all the good men gone?" I'm the pastor of a pretty large church in Florida, and from where I sit it seems like there are way more single Godly women in church than men. I'm just saying, if I was single, I'd be in our church every time the doors opened. But why the disparity? Why the ten-to-one ratio? What happened? Why is it so difficult to find a good man?

But let's back up a minute. Before we can answer that, we need to ask, "What is a man? What does it mean to be a man?" And before we dive into that, you should know a few things about me.

I love to hunt, love to fish, my favorite color's camo. I love plaid, the Georgia Bulldogs, pro golf, Braves baseball, NASCAR, sweet tea, Christensen Arms rifles, and good bourbon. I've got a beautiful wife, healthy kids, and I work out. I still have a few muscles, though not as many as I used to. When I'm not driving a four-wheel-drive Chevrolet truck, I drive my Harley. And yes, it's got highway pegs. I like cold beer, chicken wings, and nachos. And I took God literally when he said in Genesis 27:3, "Now then, take your weapons, your quiver and your bow, and go out to the field and hunt game for me." So I hunt my groceries with a Mathews bow, and I've got more guns than fingers. I could have one on me right now as I write this. Probably do.

But none of it makes me a man. It makes me awesome, but not a man. The reality is that you could be a scoop neck, skinny jeans, scarf-wearing vegan sipping an oat-milk caramel macchiato at your local hipster coffee shop—and you could be a man. It'd be a stretch, but it's possible.

Here's the truth: Whether you're married or single, every man is called to be a prophet, priest, servant king, provider, and protector. But the evidence shows that so many of us are not living up to that. Divorce is still at an all-time high, kids are growing up without dads, porn addictions are soaring, and the blame-anyone-but-me culture is runaway rampant, as is the I-got-this epidemic. We as men have not only dropped the ball, we've exited the arena. Peace out. You do you, Boo.

Where did the train leave the track? What happened? I mean, what went wrong? How in the world did we go from the apostle Paul and William Wallace and John Wayne to what we have now? Bearded fat men in dresses mocking the Lord's supper at the opening of the Olympics?

Well, there's a lot. I mean, there's a whole lot.

We could go historical. Talk about how if we were born a few hundred years ago, most of us would get up every day and go to work with our dads where we would see our dads make decisions in stewardship, in leadership, in service to others, and in hiring and firing people. Which is called discipleship. But the industrial revolution came along, and you pair that with the Great American Dream, and we see the introduction of things like the lunchbox and the La-Z-Boy. And so Dad, during the peak hours of his day, was always somewhere else.

Dad "went" to work rather than "worked" the farm. Or the store. "Work" occurred somewhere other than the home, and the family got the leftovers. And then, in one of the most tragic things that ever happened, the raising of children started to be considered women's work. Men had better, more important things to do.

And then came a world war and men primarily went off to stand in the gap against great evils that were attacking our country and attacking freedom. And when they came home, the greatest generation, who saved the world from tyranny and obliteration, often didn't know how to talk about how their best friend's face got blown off in a foxhole two feet away. War required men to switch off a part of their emotions. Otherwise, they'd have never made it. So, they saved the world, only to return home and find they couldn't just turn it back on. I'm fifty-one years old. My dad served in Vietnam, and any time I dig around and try to talk about heart matters, we eventually get to the point where he goes crickets. There's just stuff we don't talk about.

Not only do we face all those obstacles, but there's no rite of passage in our current context that makes a boy a man. During seminary, I spent a summer in Kenya, and I spent some time with the Maasai tribe. One of the tribal warriors came to me and said, "So how do you know when a boy is a man in your culture?" I thought, "Wow, that's a good question." Many think it's when they win *Fortnite* or *Halo*, or get a girl to third base.

We have no true rite of passage for when a boy becomes a man in our culture. In the Maasai culture, the boys went out and hunted lions. With spears. To become a man, they had two options: Walk through the grass until they find Mufasa, sling a spear through his chest, and then walk back into camp wearing a lion-skin coat with a big mane—or option B: miss and get eaten. Warrior or dead. Those were your two options.

In our culture, how do we know when a boy becomes a man? Obamacare says 26. Budweiser says 21. United States Army says 18. Xbox says 17. (By the way, there is no such thing as a mature video game. Just jot that down.) DMV says 16. Disney says 10. They charge you adult prices at 10 years old. The only place I can find any consistency is both Delta Air Lines and Advil. They agree, at 2 years old, you're an adult.

And because we have no shared cultural definition of manhood, and because there is no rite of passage into manhood, and because many of our men and fathers have abdicated their role in search of what's easy, painless, or comfortable, you get this thing called delayed—or prolonged—boyhood. For all of human history, until about the last fifty or sixty years, there were only two categories of male. There was a boy, and there was a man. And typically, what would happen is he would start a family, start a career, or fight in a war. Either way, you left a boy and came home a man. But in just very recent human history, a new category of male evolved. He's got one foot in boyhood while dipping a toe in manhood. Sort of checking it out. Looks a little bit like a man but still sort of a boy. Kind of a boy that can shave. In truth, it's a boy who wants the privileges of manhood without the responsibilities. He's called a dude. And let's be honest. We've got lots of "dudes."

Dudes pursue boyish things, hoping to declare manhood upon themselves. Junior gets sweet rims for his ride, mixed with a bass-pounding, eardrum-piercing stereo, throws a Glock in the glove box, and then tests the boundaries with a girl in the back seat. Where I grew up in Dillon, South Carolina, we weren't into rims. We were into monster tires, glass pack mufflers, and twelve-inch lifts. But it's the same thing.

Our society is also really impressed with consumption. With shiny things. Or at least we tell ourselves it is. I can consume more from you. More than you. More women, more beer, more drugs, more money, whatever it is. We tell ourselves and each other that my consumption makes me a man. The message is, I'm consuming, doing what men do, therefore I must be a man.

Wrong. Sorry to be blunt, but boys can technically become fathers at about twelve or thirteen, but that does not make them a man any more than putting your head in the oven makes you a biscuit. Boys chase fun and what makes them feel good rather than responsibility. They demand what they haven't earned. We live in a world of entitled boys. Immature pretenders. Boys with masks.

Here's the truth about us men. Every man that I know wants to be a man. Wants to be seen as a "real" man, and yet we live in a world that sends mixed and false signals about how to be a man or "do" manhood. It's complicated. Not easy. Add to that a spiritual enemy who desperately does not want men to act like real men, and it's pretty much a dumpster fire. As a result, if we're gut-level honest, most of us are left guessing, "What is a real man and how do I become one?"

You might be a tough mudder. World's strongest man. Run a hedge fund worth billions. An MVP pro athlete. Reigning MMA Champ. A podium CrossFitter. A points-winning Formula 1 driver. Winner of the World Series of Poker. Lead guitarist for the best rock and roll band in the world. Tatted from top-knot to toe. Have jacked arms and twelve-pack abs with 2 percent body fat. You could even be president. Winner of the Nobel Prize. Voted World's Most Interesting Man and make all the best beer commercials.

But a man? A "real" man? Truth is, you can do and be all the above and yet still be a self-centered, defiant, rebellious boy hell-bent on doing what he wants to do, when he wants to do it, however he wants to do it, and do so without ever asking anyone's permission. Least of all, God's.

A man can be and do all those incredible and noteworthy things but, contrary to popular opinion, being those things and doing those things does not make you a man. They don't define you. They're just what you get to do *as* a man. This is why nine-year-olds don't serve in the military. Just because they can play war with their friends doesn't mean we put a rifle in their hands.

There's nothing more dangerous in this world than an insecure, ungrounded man. It's what gangs are full of. It's why casinos grow larger and larger. It's why bars are open late. And think about this—almost every single nonprofit that has ever been started could be traced back to the fact that men did not do what God has called men to do. Oftentimes the reason women are in pain is because some man did not do what he was supposed to do. Or what he promised. A father, a husband, a boyfriend, leveraged his own strength for abuse instead of serving them. Or he flexed his sexual prowess in promiscuity and infidelity rather than doing what he said he would—"Be faithful to you as long as you both shall live."

Ladies, you may not know this, but there's a deep, fundamental question that every single man is wrestling with and it is this: "Do I have what it takes? I know God's called me to be a man, but do I have what it takes to be one? To become one?" (I learned this from John Eldridge.) Fundamentally, our greatest fear is that you will peel back the *S* on our chest and discover we're just a poser. A kid who bought a cape at the thrift store. That we're a fraud. A pretender. That we really don't have what it takes. That we're all just insecure little boys trying to prove ourselves.

This plays out in so many different ways. It's why we want to drive fast, or have some kind of hobby that we're way too into. It's why we want to make a bunch of money and sell stuff, and be on top, and be the best. It's why guys chase around a little white ball, like that thing really matters. You smack it around, and you're like,

"Get in the hole, ball," which more often than not is code for "Do I have what it takes?"

Why? Because we're trying to prove ourselves.

And then to make matters worse, we bet on it. We waste money on the little white ball. As if moving it around somebody's backyard and dropping it in a hole in the dirt makes us somehow better than someone else. I have several friends who are professional golfers, and they're amazing athletes who work really hard. I wish I could play like them. For sure. But, for most of us, the chest-pounding has more to do with masking something than simply enjoying what can be a beautiful game.

The authority for what constitutes a man is not the latest action flick, it's not the latest influencer with the most followers, and it's not the media. According to God, the authority is His Word. And according to the Bible, a man is defined not by what he does externally but by who he worships internally. Does he imitate Christ or not? Does he act like Jesus or some action-flick hero?

What did Christ do? Just give me the brass tacks. Well, bottom line, He laid down His life for those He loved. Without considering or acting on what he wanted. There it is. Easy-peazy. *By the one man's obedience the many will be made righteous* (Romans 5:17). You go and do likewise. By definition, you cannot stand as a man until you bend the knee and bow to the only King of all Kings. There it is. If you want to stand as a man, you must bow to the King. Period.

Straight up, manhood is bestowed. How many times have we watched a medieval movie where some guy kneels before a king and the king touches his shoulders with his sword? "Rise a knight." It's because in a loose way, manhood is bestowed in a similar way. Look at the posture of the knight. He's dressed for battle, trained in battle, capable of rescuing the girl and his sword is sharp and his horse fast, but look at what he's doing. He's bowing before his king. That's a knight. His life is spent in service and worship of the king. Period. Don't miss this—he bows before he swings his sword.

In the same way, manhood is bestowed by God when we bow before him. In worship, service, and total surrender. The point I'm trying to make is this: Most of us spend our lives trying to do manly things. Or what we think is manly based on what we watch or value. We buy fast cars, big boats, expensive watches, spend way too much time chasing little white balls, or become an aficionado of cigars or wine or whiskey. Look, I'm not against any of those things. I like them all. But acquiring them and doing them has nothing to do with being a man in the eyes of God. And His eyes are the only eyes that matter. The litmus test for manhood is this—do we imitate Christ? Do we lay down our life for those we love?

This book is about how to be a man according to God. Note I did not say, "feel like a man." Why? Well, because according to King David, your feelings will lie to you. Trust me, when you're changing a diaper, washing a sippy cup, or sitting in your minivan in the carpool line, you may not feel all that manly. That's because manhood is a heart condition before it is an external expression. It's an inward decision before it's an act. This thing in your hands is not a deodorant commercial. Not a "six steps to a better you." And we're not selling beer. This is a book about true, biblical manhood. It's about being a man of God. Which is the only kind of man there is. Every other type is a counterfeit.

It's no secret that modern-day manhood is jacked up. Massively. And there are a lot of people trying to figure out how to fix it.

One response the world pushes is to say that men and women are the same. No difference. Slight little plumbing variation, but outside of that, we're just the same. That gender is simply a function of how you "feel." That you are your own god and you get to claim what you are. Everyone knows this is a lie from the pit of hell. Listen, as smart and progressive as we are, we can't figure out where to go to the bathroom right now or what sports division to sign up for, okay? I don't think we're progressing. Men and women are not the same. We are different by design. God's design. And while I'm here, any attack on gender is, at its root, an attack on the character and nature of God. It's simple, defiant rebellion.

The opposite pendulum swing is "men and women are different, but men are better." Which is simple chauvinism. And it has no place in the church, and it has nothing to do with the gospel of Jesus Christ. The church has to reject both of those lies and teach the truth of the gospel.

The church, historically, at least in the last forty or fifty years, has not helped very much when it comes to defining manhood. Do you know why most churches don't have a lot of men in them? Because in a lot of churches, the common message is, "Hey, to be a Christian man, you really need to be more like women."

Right? Am I wrong? When men show up at church and ask, "What do you do here at this church?" the answer is "Well, we read a lot. You can join the choir. And we like to sit in circles and talk about our feelings. Fundamentally, we want you to sit down, be quiet, and behave." And men are thinking, *Well, if that's what it is, then I don't think I'm going to that. I'd rather play golf.* And I don't blame them. I wouldn't go, either. Maybe that's why we started our church, but that's another book.

And so let me tell you this: To be a Christian, to be a follower of Jesus Christ, does not mean that you have to check your testicles at the door. That's right, I said it. Given the abuses of some of those who've come before us, we're often made to place them on the chopping block and walk out emasculated. Which is a crock.

Being a man is a great, high calling, but God did not give you that strength for your own self. He didn't give it to you so you could pound your chest and scream, "I got this." Truth is, you don't, never have, and never will. If you're a male made in God's image, then He gave you manhood for His Glory and for the provision and protection of everybody He put around you. This may be news to some of you, but ultimately, being a man is a selfless calling.

In 1 Corinthians 16:13–14, it says, "Be watchful, stand firm in the faith, act like men, be strong. Let all that you do be done in love."

Ephesians 6:13–14 says, "Therefore take up the whole armor of God, that you may be able to withstand in the evil day, and having done all, to stand firm. Stand therefore."

You starting to see a pattern? It says *stand* four times in two verses.

Men, let me say this: Make no apologies for being a man. We have that 1 Corinthians verse written in the bathroom at our church. You've got to read something while you're in there. Might as well read the Bible.

Think of it this way: The core command "Act like men" is the hub of the wheel. Everything depends on that. Without it, there's no wheel. Nothing happens.

The imperatives around it are our marching orders that grow out of the hub. The spokes. They are the "doing" of the stand-firm part. It's how we are to pull standing. We're going to explore both the hub and the spokes in this book.

The reality is we live in a world right now that wants you to apologize for being a man. To sit down. Because your mere presence triggers someone and makes them want to dive into a safe space.

Make no apologies.

And right about here is where most men come off the rails. I say, "Make no apologies," and guys translate that into doing abusive, dumb, manipulative, controlling, fear-causing stuff. We become jerks.

We flex our muscles, raise our voice, stand on our platform and pound our chest, and abuse what God's given us. A bunch of women have been bruised because some dude went to a men's conference and came home with his face painted blue, waving a five-foot sword screaming, "Freedom!" and thinking he was going to right every wrong, only to run over the woman in the process.

Look, I'm all for *Braveheart*. Lord knows I love that movie. Got a replica sword mounted on the wall of my office. But don't forget the ending—William Wallace laid down his life for a people. For a country. He lived a life that said *Your stuff is more important than my stuff*. Which is the heart of Christ. A life laid down for us.

I'm not telling you to act like a moron. I'm telling you to make no apology for God's sovereign intention in your life for His Glory. The Bible says the Lord is a warrior, the Lord is His name. And you have been created in His image. And we live in a world that does not want us to be men. And certainly not a warrior. Actually, it wants women to be men and men to be women. Every kid's movie that my children watched growing up depicts the dad as an idiot, and the hamster saves the day. You do not have to check your man card to follow after Jesus Christ. In fact, you can't be a man until you bend that knee and follow Him. It's a prerequisite. No, it's *the* prerequisite. The good news of the gospel is that in God's kingdom you don't have to check your man card and you don't have to mask who you are. And the moment you realize that in and of yourself you don't have what it takes but that the God of the universe actually thought you up and custom-made you, then you are precisely ready to stand up and act like a man.

How many of us believe in something so much that we would be willing to let some sick miscreant tie us to a table and disembowel us in front of our friends and family rather than renounce the thing or ones we love? Because that's the freedom Wallace fought for. To die free. A slave of no tyrant king.

Let me ask it this way: How many of us would let some sick miscreant strap us to a post and then scourge us until we became unrecognizable as a man—having lost most of the skin and flesh from our neck, back, and sides—and then force-march us out of town and nail us naked to a tree on a public road, where we would eventually drown in our own lung fluid? Any takers?

Biblical manhood is not easy. It's also not real popular. But it is commanded to those of us who follow Jesus. If you're reading this, then chances are good you're a follower of Jesus and you're wanting to follow Him more closely. Great. I'm glad you're here. Or, you're testing this idea of following Jesus. You've heard some stories and you're wondering what those guys have that you don't. Glad you're here. Or maybe lastly, you're not too sure about the whole Jesus thing but you're looking at your life and you've really messed up and based on your record you have very little idea of what being a man really is. No problem. There's room for all of us around the feet of Jesus. And what you'll learn once you've been here a minute is that all of us have the same skeletons in our closets, we all walk with the same limp, all share the same insecurities and fears and screwups and wish-I-hadn't-done-thats. Not one of us has the monopoly on this. You're in good company. Just look around you.

Here's my encouragement. Don't skim this. Hang in there. I'm going to say some hard things to you. So, swallow your pride. Buck up. You can take it. I'm not poking you in the chest to keep you down. I'm locking arms with you to raise you up. Into the man God created you to be. To do that, we need to hold up a mirror and realize that if we really want to follow Jesus, it means we do what He did. Follow where He leads. Jesus was and is the greatest man to ever live. He's the model. The plumbline. So we're going to look at what He said and did and then ask Him to help us do that.

Let me say one thing before I move on: When I say He was the greatest man to ever live, He was. Period. Hands down. Mic drop.

But, He was also, at the exact same time, simultaneously, God. One hundred percent man and 100 percent God. Do I completely understand that? No. Can I make sense of how that's possible? Not really. Can I really wrap my head around how the God of the universe, the King of all Kings, could stoop down and allow Himself to become fully man? Or as the Bible says, "put on flesh"? Nope. I can't. But I believe with every cell in my body that He did. I take it on faith.

So with Jesus as the model, my hope is to walk you through what scripture says to you and me about manhood. And as I do that, I'm going to use a bunch of other scriptures to help us understand the first one. This is called using scripture to interpret itself. My process here is not complicated and what the Bible has to say is pretty simple. Which is good because we're all sheep and if you know anything about them, they're not all that smart. And not to point out the obvious, but they're totally lost without their shepherd. The difficult part is not the understanding or the hearing, but the doing. More about that later.

And while this is a book for men, it's equally for any woman who is married to a man, dating a man, wanting to date a man, raising a future man, going to church with men, or loves a man. Mommas, wives, girlfriends—please keep reading. Chances are about 100 percent that God will use you to draw your man further into manhood. Before you start feeling left out, thinking I'm just adding to your list of stuff to do, please don't. I've written this book with you in mind as well. I pray it encourages you. And maybe even helps you know how to better pray for the men in your life. I hope it will.

And let me say this before the enemy whispers in your ear—for all you single mommas whose man ran out on you, and you're looking at your boy and scratching your head, don't lose heart. You too can grow him into a man. Just point him to Jesus, and tough love won't kill him. God is good. We are for you. You have what it takes. And I praise God for the single momma who lays down her life for her children. Your crown in heaven will be beautiful to see. You keep raising your boys into men. You are not alone. We are pulling for you. God is with you. And yes, God will give you everything you need and use you—that's right, you—to raise your boy into a man. And as much as I'm for single mommas, it's not supposed to be that way. That is not God's intention. Failed dads are the enemy's plan and a result of the Fall. In fact, the overwhelming majority of the problems that we face in our country can be traced back to fatherlessness in the home. Absent dads. Dudes.

For all you Type As, here it is in brass tacks—we're going to walk through what the Bible means when it says, *Be watchful, stand firm, be strong, and let all that you do be done in love* (1 Cor. 16:13–14), and then we're going to ask ourselves some tough questions.

Questions like: What would it look like for me to actually do that? What if I really stood firm on the Word of God, unwavering? What if I actually believed, like way down in my gut, what it said and then did it? And what if I really loved others the way Jesus loved me? If I just did these simple things, what kind of man would I be?

I started this book by telling you the story of my failed canoe trip and how grateful we were to see that old man towing our boat back upriver along with all our stuff. I've got a few more years on me than many of you, along with a few more gray hairs and wrinkles. I've been here a minute and got a few scars. This doesn't mean I know everything, but it does mean I've made some mistakes and learned a few things. I am entitled to an opinion.

WHERE HAVE ALL THE GOOD MEN GONE?

And here's my opinion: Most of you have canoe-wrecked your lives and you need an old man to help get you out of the mess you've created. In our church, we have an elder named Dr. Paul. He's a giant of the faith. Used to run the medical school at LSU, among other things. Five years ago, when he was eighty-five years old, folks asked me to stop him from running around the world doing mission work. This never made sense to me.

"Why?"

Their response was always the same. "He might die."

"So?" I mean, can you think of a better way to go? And "retirement" is an American concept, not a biblical one. Just ask Moses and Aaron.

Dr. Paul is now ninety years old, and this year he's going back to Africa. On mission. Why? Because he never got off mission. He's still on it. Still in love with his wife, Sally. Still in love with the Bride of Christ. Still discipling guys like me. Still laying down his life for the gospel of Jesus Christ so that one more might be added to the kingdom. He is not sitting on the couch covered in Cheetos talking about the good ol' days.

Now to be sure, we're taking care of him. Another doctor is going with him. We're rolling out the red carpet. Doing everything we can to help and assist.

But Dr. Paul stood up a long time ago, and by the Grace of God, he's still standing firm and acting like God's man. He has no intention of sitting down or sitting this one out.

My goal is to be ninety years old and still on mission.

So let's you and I dive in and really ask God to help us understand what it means to stand up and act like a man, and then let's do that. Let me pray for you.

Our good and gracious heavenly Father. I thank You for sending Your perfect Son, the second person of the Trinity, Jesus Christ, on a rescue mission for all men and women. Thank You, Jesus, that You would humble Yourself and put on flesh. That You, while never setting aside your divinity, willfully stepped out of heaven and lived as a man. A perfect man. The God-man. Thank You that You humbled Yourself and became a servant. A servant of mankind for anyone who would believe that You even were obedient to death on a cross that we might be saved. God, Your word tells us that our attitude should be the same as that of Christ Jesus. The perfect man was humble and obedient. He was fierce and tender. He was strong and empathetic. He spoke and the demons trembled, and He also wept with His friends in times of tragedy. God, Your Word says that we are predestined to be formed in the image of Your Son, Jesus. That means that in order for us to Stand Firm and Act Like Men, we must first admit that we can't do this on our own. We must believe that when Jesus pushed up on His nail-pierced feet and screamed, "It is finished," that counted for us. And WE must confess Christ as our LORD if we are to walk in His footsteps. Father, it is a high and holy calling that You would call us to stand up and act like men. By the power of the Holy Spirit in us, in accordance with the truth of God's Word guiding us, we ask that You lead us to Stand Firm and Act Like Men. We have no idea what hangs in the balance for our world and for those that we love the most.

Amen.

DOING THE STUFF

At the end of each chapter, I'm going to give you something to do. Some action to take other than passively sitting there and reading this book. I call it "doing the stuff." Why? Because many of us need to get up off the couch, brush off the Cheetos, and do the stuff of being a man.

This does not mean pound our chest like a silverback. It means to bow, and the first thing we're going to do as we bow before the King and His throne is treasure His Word and write it on our hearts.

This is why the Psalmist says in Psalm 119:11, "I have stored up your word in my heart, that I might not sin against you." Seems like a lot of us would all be in much better places if we'd started doing that a long time ago. Can I get a witness? So, your first action step is pretty simple. Not all that complicated. It's pretty low-hanging fruit.

I want you to write 1 Corinthians 16:13–14 and Ephesians 6:13–14 on a card and put it in your wallet or money clip or inside your phone case. All you overachievers can laminate it, which is probably a good idea. Just put it somewhere you'll see it on a daily basis as a reminder. And we've made it easy for you. We printed it early on in this book. So, write it down, keep it with you, and start reading it out loud to yourself. Commit it to memory. Spend ninety seconds memorizing rather than scrolling TikTok. Trust me, it's much better for you.

Chapter 1

WHAT IS A MAN?

Then God said, "Let us make man in our image, after our likeness. And let them have dominion over the fish of the sea and over the birds of the heavens and over the livestock and over all the earth and over every creeping thing that creeps on the earth." So God created man in his own image, in the image of God he created him; male and female he created them. And God blessed them. And God said to them, "Be fruitful and multiply and fill the earth and subdue it, and have dominion over the fish of the sea and over the birds of the heavens and over every living thing that moves on the earth."

—Genesis 1:26-28

Everyone knows that before you build a house, you pour the foundation. And one size doesn't fit all. You don't just pour two inches of concrete and then erect eighty stories on top of it and call it a day. The depth of the foundation, or thickness of the concrete, depends entirely on what's going on top of it. Cutting corners on the foundation will always come back to bite you in the long run. No one in their right mind would buy the penthouse suite in a high-rise if they knew the foundation was only six inches deep. We take it for granted that shortcuts in construction are always a bad idea. One hundred percent of the time. It's the stuff beneath the surface that you can't see that matters most. Not the decoration.

Same can be said of trees. Tall trees require deep tap roots, otherwise they topple in wind and wither in drought. No staying power. They are incapable of standing firm.

We all agree to this, but when it comes to manhood, boys are cutting corners left and right. Few want to put in the time to pour a rock-solid base.

One summer, I was standing in the weight room with my son's football team during early-morning workouts. It was a bunch of high schoolers looking pretty standing around talking. Nobody really getting after it. As if standing in the weight room would somehow mysteriously put muscle on them.

Now in order to understand what I'm about to say, you need to know something about me: I was once a pretty dedicated bodybuilder. I lived in the weight room. But it's not like I was all show and no go. I once bench-pressed five hundred pounds—in competition. Now, I'm not saying that to brag, although I'm proud of the accomplishment, but it's so that you understand I know a thing or two about what it takes to grow muscle.

So, as I stood there in the weight room watching everybody watch everybody else, I got a little excited and used my grown-up voice: "Everybody wants to be strong! Nobody wants to be sore!"

That's us. We want the benefit without the pain. The growth without the sweat. But getting stronger requires intentionally putting yourself in pain and under duress day after day after day for incremental and often unseen gains.

All of this means that to understand God's intention for manhood, we need to go all the way back to Genesis, so we get to the foundation or the root of what we're talking about here.

In Genesis 1:26–27, God says, *"Let us make mankind in our image and likeness." So male and female, he created them.* Here's what this means. God is a triune God. There's one God and three persons. God the Father, Son, and Holy Spirit. And God's love for God's self spills out onto creation, and He creates an image bearer. But man alone was not enough. That word "image" in the original Hebrew is a masculine word. The word "likeness" is a feminine word. So he makes male and female. Don't miss this. The God of this universe, and every other, made man and He made woman. To bear His image. Reflect Him. And He did so out of and through a limitless love.

This means females alone were not enough to image God correctly. And males alone are not enough to image God correctly. But in the garden and all throughout history when men and women, when male and female, when husband and wife come together in one, it is the closest thing to a complete image of God that we have here on earth.

And so after God had spoken everything into existence, the Bible says this in chapter 2 verses 5–7: "When no bush of the field was yet in the land and no small plant of the field had yet sprung up—for the LORD God had not caused it to rain on the land, and there was no man to work the ground, and a mist was going up from the land and was watering the whole face of the ground—then the LORD God formed the man." Men, God formed you. Intentionally. He took the time to think you up. What you see in the mirror started in the mind and heart of God. He spoke into existence the stars, but when it came to you, He fashioned and formed you on purpose. And, of the nine billion or so people on planet Earth, there's only one you. Again, don't ever apologize for being the man that God has created you to be. Now, I'm not saying that to give you license to pound your chest as a tyrant in your home. If you do, you've missed the point entirely.

And so, he formed the man of the dust of the ground, and he breathed into his nostrils the breath of life. And the man became a living creature (v. 7). Watch what happens here. God fashioned man by hand from the dust, then closed His lips over the man's nostrils and breathed in the "ruach" of God. This Hebrew word means "breath, spirit, and life." It means all three. Now step back a minute. When did the dust become a man? When God breathed into him.

Some of you have the appearances of a man, the shape of a man, but in reality, you're the shell of a male. You've never really received the breath of God. My prayer for you as you read this is that God would breathe his ruach, His Spirit, the breath of life, in you. That you would open your eyes for the very first time and come face-to-face with your heavenly Father, and in response, you would bow before the King. Because only after you have can you step up and be the man that God has called you to be. Now watch what God does next. Verse 8: "And the LORD God planted a garden in Eden, in the east, and there he put the man whom he had formed." Notice the man was not created in the garden. He was created in the wilderness. God created him in the wilderness and then placed him in the garden. We're gonna see in a little while that the woman was created in the garden. This matters.

You know the reason you have this warrior thing stirring in you? If you've got little children, this is where it hits the clearest. I have a boy and a girl. They are not the same. Every stick that falls out of a tree is a princess wand to my daughter. It is a bazooka to my son. Every pine cone that falls to the ground is a grenade. That's just who he is. A little warrior. Today, he's training MMA. I've got to be careful when I hug him that he doesn't choke me out. This dichotomy between boys and girls makes some of you super uncomfortable. You don't let your kids have toy guns. "Timmy can't have a toy gun. That's so dangerous. I don't want him growing up to just be one more angry man." So you take away every stick. And yet when lunch rolls around and you make him a grilled cheese, he will chew it into a Glock and point it at his sister. And you ask, "Ah. Does he have issues?"

His issue is that God made the boy to grow up to be a man who protects and defends. It's wrapped around our DNA. God put it there. You can deny it, you can try and stuff it or repress it, you can ignore it or even castigate it, but the defender instinct is in there whether you like it or not, and it will always be there. And we need those little boys with toy guns to grow up and trade in their Nerf guns for the real thing to stand on that wall to protect us from evil and push back darkness.

For Christmas one year, I got my son a machete. That's right, a machete. My wife Gretchen was like, "Really? You think a machete is a good idea?" I think JP was seven. I'm thinking, "Baby, what could go wrong?"

Now, for the record, I didn't just give it to him and let him shove it in his backpack on his way to school. We worked with it. I showed him how and when to use it. He and I cut stuff down, together. He learned the value of it and the danger of it. And when he got older and learned to respect it, I let him keep it in his room. This process took a few years. But I wasn't just training his hands, I was training his heart. He received his first firearm the following year.

Verse 9. "And out of the ground the LORD God made to spring up every tree that is pleasant to the sight and good for food. The Tree of Life was in the midst of the garden, and the tree of the knowledge of good and evil." The next few verses mention all these rivers. Why? I think God gave us its location to let us know that the garden was real.

But when we get to verse 15, God gives Adam, the very first man, three things under the context of one banner. And these matter, a lot.

The first thing that he gives Adam is this: "The LORD God took the man and put him in the Garden of Eden to work it and keep it." First thing that God gave Adam, the very first man, is work to enjoy. This is before the Fall. Adam has yet to sin, so work is not a result of sin. Not a punishment. I want you to see this—before there was sin, there was work. Why am I hammering this point? Because, man, you were created to work. God invites Adam (and in a little while, he's going to invite Eve, too) to be a cocreator in his creation. He gets Eden started, but then he looks at Adam and says, *Join me in this. There's still a lot of work I want you to do. Starting with subdue and cultivate.* Now compare this to us in the present day. Most of us work really hard not to have to work. It's backward. Upside down. This is not a biblical value. The word "retirement" occurs nowhere in scripture. Now, will there come a day when maybe we don't go to the same job we've been going to for thirty years? Of course. But this is what I mean. Remember Dr. Paul? Turning ninety and returning to Africa on mission. Note: He didn't just plant himself in a La-Z-Boy and start flipping through TV channels. He could have, and who could argue? He's earned it. But Dr. Paul is passionate about building God's kingdom and not his own, so he didn't. Since his "retirement," he has poured himself into discipling young men in our church. He has been and continues to cultivate disciples. In some ways, he has worked harder since his "retirement" from medicine.

In the garden, work was rearranging the raw goods that God had provided for human flourishing. That's what work was. The same thing is true today. This is why I don't believe there is a secular-sacred divide in our vocation. In other words, I don't think my job is holy because I work in a church, and your job is not because you work wherever you work. This is why men need a calling within a career more than a job. Can this be difficult to find? Of course. But rather than cry out to God and seek His face to know your calling, some of you whine about it, play the victim, and use the excuse "I just don't think I'm called to that" to skirt responsibility.

Look, Scooter, here's what you're called to. You're called to work. So, if you don't know your calling, get you a job so you can work while you're figuring out the calling piece. Oftentimes, God will use your obedience in the not-knowing to call you into His plan for you. Why? Sometimes I think it's because He wants to know if you'll follow Him even when you don't understand. Again, our job—our work—according to God, is to rearrange the raw goods He has provided for human flourishing. That may mean you take sticks and stones, and you arrange them into a home so that families can be created there. That may mean you rearrange the raw goods of medicine so that you can accomplish the will of God by bringing human healing into the lives of people. That may mean you help people steward their finances through banking or wealth management. It may mean you teach our children. Preach. Make art for His glory and our joy. Or it may mean you landscape yards, engineer cities, or fly planes safely to ferry the rest of us around the world.

Whatever it is, we—men—are supposed to go to work. Sitting around, doing nothing, is not and never has been a biblical value. Now are there times of rest, sabbath, and rejuvenation? Sure. And thank God. But we are resting from work so that we can get back to it. Not so that we don't have to work.

Listen, we have a good dad who invites His children to go to work with Him. This is what I mean—have you ever asked your kid to help you with a project? How much help are they? Ever asked your six-year-old to help you repair the irrigation? Or change the brakes on Mom's van? Plunge the toilet? How much help is he?

None. Absolutely zero. If we're honest, he's a hindrance more than a help. And yet, don't you enjoy it when they crawl underneath the van and ask, "Can I help?" Of course you do. This is exactly what God is inviting us to do. Join Him in His work. Number one, He gives us work to enjoy.

When I was in college, I had my sights set on going to medical school. Despite the fact that most accuse me of sounding like Larry the Cable Guy in the pulpit, I actually made really good grades and was accepted into medical school. I thought I'd spend the rest of my life as a doctor. Somewhere in here God did a thing in my heart and I knew that I wasn't supposed to go to medical school. How did I know? Can't really say other than I knew that God had called me to ministry. Which meant I needed to have a conversation with my dad and tell him that I would not be going to medical school after all, but instead to seminary to be trained to be a youth pastor. The conversation went over like a lead balloon. My dad was not impressed.

"What's a seminary?"

"It's preacher school."

He said, "Preacher school? Why? They only study one book and only work a half a day a week. Why would you need a school for that?"

I let him know that ministry was a legit career and that I believed God was calling me to make disciples of teenagers as my full-time job. My dad replied, "Boy—you don't get up and go to fun. You get up and go to work."

That should be in the Proverbs. His perception was that I was trading hard work for easy street. And I get it. It was a bit of a U-turn from where I'd told him I was going, but the truth was, I wasn't chasing fun. I was following God's call on my life. Trying to follow Jesus. To be obedient.

To this day, my dad is one of my greatest fans. And after thirty years, God—through His grace—used my life and words in ministry (along with a lot of other people praying and sowing into him) to bring my dad into the Kingdom of God. My dad surrendered his life to the Lordship of Jesus. Would that have happened if I were an orthopedist? Probably not. But there's also great truth in what he said. Most boys, when choosing a career, look for the fun, for what is comfortable, for what makes them look good in other people's eyes, or what lets them feel the way they want to feel because that's how they want to feel—which is a great definition of a dude—rather than choosing what is uncomfortable or what will test them. The difference between men and boys is simple: Boys choose situations where they can control the outcome, men risk failure.

Bottom line: God gave us work to enjoy, and working in your calling is never drudgery. It has been and remains one of the great joys of my life.

Second thing, verses 16–17: "And the LORD God commanded the man, saying, 'You may surely eat of every tree of the garden, but of the tree of the knowledge of good and evil you shall not eat, for in the day that you eat of it you shall surely die.'" The second thing that God gives Adam is a will to obey. He gives him work to enjoy and a will to obey. Now, check this out. God was not into rules; God was into relationship. There is only one Thou Shalt Not in the Garden of Eden. There was only one No, and there were a lot of Yeses. *Eat from any tree, just stay away from that one* (vv. 16–17). God is a good God. Do you know what some of the commandments were? They were: Enjoy the garden. Eat of all these other trees. And then there's this one—be fruitful and multiply. That's Hebrew for bow-chicka-wow-wow. Praise God. That was God's idea. To which all of us would say, "I love the commandments."

The one No God gives says, *There's this thing over here that will kill you. I love you enough to warn you to stay away from that thing.* Why? Because He loves us. Period. So He gives us work to enjoy, He gives us will to obey.

Then verse 18: "Then the Lord God said, 'It is not good that the man should be alone; I will make him a helper fit for him.'" So the third thing he gives to Adam is a woman to love. In short, the three *W*'s: work to enjoy, will to obey, and a woman to love. (I think the first time I heard it explained this way was from Jon Tyson at an Acts29 conference more than ten years ago.)

Now, if you're single, let me talk to you real quick. God intends the 99.99999 percent of you to get married. But to the less than 1 percent, God has given you the gift of singleness so that you would allocate all of your time, effort, and attention toward the bride of Christ. The church. If you have this gift, you probably know it. Paul had it, so it puts you in good company. And it is a gift. Now, there are some of you out there watching the clock tick and wondering if God's given you the gift of singleness because you have no spouse and no prospects. And if you're honest, you're praying, "Lord, please don't give me the gift of singleness. If you have, I'd like to exchange it for a spouse." It's a good prayer. Keep praying it. In the meantime, single men, love your momma, your sister, and especially your sisters here at church, because the way you practice will determine how you play. And if you cannot love, honor, and respect every female that God puts into your life, then there's no way that one day you're going to put on a tux, stand at an altar, make a promise, and all of a sudden be able to love, honor, and respect her. Never going to happen. God's intention is for you to have a woman to love. So stop denigrating and stealing from His daughters.

Ladies, I need you to see this. See right here where it says, "I will make a helper fit for him"? Remember, men are sheep and we can be really dumb, so we need your help. That word "helper" is in no way denigrating of women. The Hebrew word is "Ezer" and is used dozens of times in the Old Testament. The majority of the time it is used to describe God as the "helper" to Israel.

First, let me tell you some ways to not try to help. Don't bring up this book to your husband at all unless he initiates it. You are not his Holy Spirit. He doesn't need you to put him under your thumb. This means don't start dinner on Wednesday with "Well, when you gonna do the stuff Pastor Joby was talking about?" This is not helpful.

Also, if your man is reading this and has half a brain, sometime in the next seven days, he is going to start stepping into spaces that maybe he hasn't been to in a long time. He's going to risk some stuff. And when he does, please, please, please don't try to correct him. Encourage him. Don't point out his mistakes. Praise progress.

I know some of you are like, "Listen, you hadn't taken me on a date since the 1900s. Now you're trying to take me on seven, and I gained twelve pounds at the Olive Garden. I ain't dumb. The only reason you're doing that is 'cause Pastor Joby said so in his book."

Just relax a minute, darling, right. Give us some space. You don't really come with a manual, and none of us have got this figured out. We're going to make a few mistakes. A bunch, really. Please, no matter what he does, or tries to do, let this be your response. You ready? "Hercules, Hercules." That's it. If you miss the Disney movie reference, ask your kids.

I cannot put into words the power of encouragement from a woman. There's really no equal. I'm a relatively successful person, and I've run a lot of ministries. Every week when I preach, people should write down things I say. But do you know when I feel like the man? When my wife can't get the lid off the jelly jar, and she hands that thing to me, and I go, "There you go, baby." And your man needs that, too. Even when he tries dumb stuff. He needs your encouragement. Truth is, us men are like puppies. We repeat what is rewarded. So if he gets it right one time, give him a treat, and he'll be like, "Golly, I should do that again."

Now look at verses 19–20: "Now out of the ground the Lord God had formed every beast of the field and every bird of the heavens and brought them to the man to see what he would call them. And whatever the man called every living creature, that was its name. The man gave names to all livestock and to the birds of the heavens and to every beast of the field. But for Adam there was not found a helper fit for him."

Can you see the picture? God creates all the animals and tells Adam to name them. Which is cool. It's the first order in establishing dominion. Now look at Adam in that process. One by one the animals parade by, and each time he's left scratching his head. Why? Because they all have a mate save him. He's alone.

At first, I think he's very descriptive in the naming. He's like, "Hippopotamus and rhinoceros, and duck-billed platypus." But pretty soon, he's like, "Lord, this ain't doing it for me. Rat, gnat, cat. You know, can we move on?"

Why? Because there is not a helper suitable for him. Then we get to verse 21. "So the Lord God caused a deep sleep to fall upon the man, and while he slept took one of his ribs and closed up its place with flesh."

Couple things that are very important. You've been to enough weddings to know that a part of the reason God took the rib was because they were gonna be side by side in their ministry in life. Forever. Coequals under God.

Also, single men, this is very important. Notice the order. Adam named the animals and got everything ordered in his life. *Then* God gave him a wife. A lot of guys have asked me, "When is God gonna give me a woman?"

And my response is this: "Hey, if you were God, would you give you one of His daughters? You live at your mom's house. And she's still doing your laundry. Move out. Get your own place. Order your life. Take responsibility for yourself instead of rolling it off onto other people." A lot of people don't know this, and I'm not saying this to make it about me, but when I was first getting into ministry, and beginning to feel the very real weight of ministry, I used to pray, "Lord, please don't lighten my load. Give me broader shoulders." Maybe you should pray that.

Straight up, "What would you do if He gave you a girl?"

And some of you immature dudes would reply. "I know what I would do if I had a girl." Okay, Scooter, when that ninety seconds is up, what about the rest your life? Do you have your world in order to the extent that you can invite her into it? The better question is, what have you done to show Him that He can trust you with one of His most precious creations? His daughter. The way we like to say it around my church is this: "Instead of looking for the one, why don't you become the one that the one you're looking for is looking for?" Which means take responsibility. Get a job. And get that will to obey in order. And then maybe you are ready to provide, protect, and be a prophet, priest, and king.

If you'll look in the text, you'll see that the next phrases are indented, and they have quotation marks. This means that the Bible translators want us to know that Adam is singing. Why? Because when he sees his wife, he breaks into song. This is the first R&B song in human history right here.

And the man said, "This is at last bone of my bones, flesh of my flesh. And she shall be called woman, because she was taken out of man" (v. 23). In Hebrew, the word for "woman" and "mine" are basically the same word. So here's what this means: Adam sees a dog, he's like, "Labrador." He sees a cat, "cat." A monkey, "monkey." He sees his naked wife, and he starts singing, "Mine!" But not in the way you think. Not in a possessive, owning way. But in a *we are going to be together* way. Where I come from, we'd say he calls shotgun on Eve. "I'm riding with you." Or, "Dibs."

"Therefore, a man shall leave his father and mother and hold fast to his wife" (v. 24). The King James Version says, *Leave and cleave, and they shall become one flesh.* In God's economy, in marriage, one man plus one woman equals one marriage for one lifetime. "And the man and his wife were both naked and were not ashamed" (v. 25). The older I get, the more amazing that scripture becomes. If you have yet to reach fifty, this won't make much sense, but your time is coming. Just wait.

Now, here's the thing: Notice the order. They leave and cleave, and then they're naked and unashamed. They get married, then they're naked and unashamed. In our culture, we get it backward. A lot of people get naked, then they get married, and that's why a bunch of shame, conflict, and dysfunction gets brought into your marriage. Now if this is you, don't hang your head. We're all sinners at the feet of Jesus, and each of us needs a savior to do for us what we can't do for ourselves.

But let's be honest, if you two brought sexual sin into your marriage, it's sin and God demands repentance. So, have you confessed it? Have you repented? Look, there is healing. There is restoration. There is forgiveness. God makes all things new. If I'm speaking to you, see my previous book, *Run Over by the Grace Train*. At the end of chapter 4, there's a prayer to repent for and ask God to heal sexual sin. I encourage the two of you to pray it together. Out loud. If you can't pray it together, then pray it alone; or if you've got someone you trust who won't judge you, pray it with them. The enemy loves sexual sin because he can shame us with it. So, open the door, shine a light, and don't let the enemy keep you in chains.

Also notice that the Bible says that the man is to leave his family and cleave unto his wife. In other words, when you get married, that is your new family. Your family of origin, your mom and dad and siblings, become your extended family. And your new family is the family of a husband and a wife. And if God decides to bless you with children, then you will be adding to your new family, not starting one. Your family starts the moment you say, "I do." Make sure you leave and cleave.

So, God gives Adam three things: work to enjoy, a will to obey, and a woman to love, all under the banner of worship. But here's the thing, there is no scheduled worship service in the Garden of Eden. It's not like they get together every other Tuesday and sing "Kumbaya" to God. Their entire life was worship with God. The way that they lived when they obeyed His will, the way that they worked together, when they subdued and cultivated, the way that they loved one another, was all worship. Because it honored and glorified God. It was a perfect plan and system, and things went exceedingly well for a half inch of space in your Bible. Less than one sentence.

And then, we screw it up.

Genesis 3:1 says, "Now the serpent was more crafty than any other beast of the field that the LORD God had made. He said to the woman, 'Did God actually say...'"

Stop right there. This is how the enemy always starts, because the enemy is the father of lies. And what the enemy wants you to do is to believe your doubts and doubt your beliefs. You should underline that. The enemy has been trying since this moment in the garden to get you to believe your doubts and doubt your beliefs. He wants to sneak in there and say, "Are you sure about that? Did God actually say? Is that what the Bible means? I know it says that, but that's not what it means."

Look closely at what the serpent says: "Did God actually say, 'You shall not eat of any tree in the garden'?" If you look at God's actual command to Adam in chapter 2 you'll see that God says, *"You are free to eat from any tree in the garden except for the tree in the middle of the garden."* Notice He starts with what we are free to do. The devil wants you to think that God is a God of *you can't*. But whenever God tells us not to, He does so for our own freedom, not our imprisonment. "And the woman said to the serpent, 'We may eat of the fruit of the trees in the garden, but God said, "You shall not eat of the fruit of the tree that is in the midst of the garden, neither shall you touch it, lest you die""" (vv. 2–3).

Note that God didn't say that last part. Eve added that. Why? Classic legalism. We add to what God has said because we want to make ourselves righteous in His sight. Which is rooted in pride and is, by definition, self-righteousness. If it were really possible to add to what God said, it would mean we are gods and we don't need him. "But the serpent said to the woman, 'You will not surely die. For God knows that when you eat of it your eyes will be opened, and you will be like God, knowing good and evil'" (v. 4).

The primary lie the enemy wants you to believe is that God is not for you. Ultimately, he wants you to think that God is not a good Father, and He does not love you, and that you would make a better god than He would. The enemy wants you to believe what you've suspected all along—you're alone, God doesn't care, and if your life is going to go your way, you better take matters into your own hands. Which is a lie from the pit of hell.

In my church, we sing that "Good, Good Father" song a lot. Why? Because if we could know those two things—that He is good, and that He is our Father—how different our lives would be.

WHAT IS A MAN?

What would we worry about? Name one thing. You can't. How do I know this? Because He demonstrated His love for us in this, that while we were yet still sinners, Christ died for us. God loves you, and Jesus is the proof. He's a good dad. He loves his kids. That's just who He is. Regardless of what my current circumstances are like, that's just who He is. If I knew that I knew that He loved me, that He demonstrated that love once and for all on the cross, and there was nothing I could do to ever change that, then my identity would begin to change. And that when my identity is found in the fact that He is my Father and I am His child, then everything changes. If we know and believe these two truths, the enemy is powerless against our mind.

Genesis 3:6 says, "So when the woman saw that the tree was good for food—" which is called lust of the flesh "—and that it was a delight to the eyes—" which is called lust of the eyes "—and that the tree was to be desired to make one wise—" which is called the pride of life "—she took of its fruit and ate, and she also gave some to her husband who was **with her**" (emphasis added).

The most damning preposition in all of masculinity is right here in the Bible. It's the preposition "with." Most of my life, when I read this story I thought Adam was out, like polishing his ski boat or hanging in a deer stand, or doing something real manly. Killing or grilling or maybe building a deck. But the Bible says, "who was with her." Literally in Hebrew, the preposition "im" can be translated as "elbow to elbow." This means Adam was standing right there. Watching it happen.

And there we have it. The number one problem in all of manhood. Passivity. The reason we got to where we are is not because the man actively did something wrong. It's not because he stormed the wrong castle. It's because he didn't do anything at all. Why are we passive? Because many of us are afraid of what our wives will say to us if we open our mouths. Look, I'm not afraid of much. I'm not. If I'm honest, I like a good argument. I'm not bad with words. More than that, when I was younger, I liked a good fight. Used to like taking a few just to get me warmed up. Today, in meetings, I have to sometimes dial myself back because I can be a little too truthful, and the truth without grace is a double-edged sword if we're not careful. Which makes it bloody. Which is not good in relationships. Point being, I'm not passive.

I can stand up to pretty much anyone, but when I get home, and walk in my door, I can be terrified of the opinion of the five-foot-seven, one-hundred-and-none-of-your-business-pound girl that I'm married to. It's just true. We care what our wives think and say, which is often the reason we say nothing.

"Then the eyes of both were opened, and they knew that they were naked. And they sewed fig leaves together and made themselves loincloths" (v. 7). And right here, religion is born. You see, everybody rejects God. We either reject God in the rebellion of the fruit, or we reject God in the religion of the fig leaf. We either say, "I'm eating the fruit even though you said stay away from it," or we say, "God, I don't need your son's righteousness. I'll just cover up my own sin and shame by the works of my own hands."

Then verses 8–9: "And they heard the sound of the Lord God walking in the garden in the cool of the day, and the man and his wife hid themselves from the presence of the Lord God among the trees of the garden." This is classic manhood move: duck, cover, blame. "But the Lord God called to the man and said to him, 'Where are you?'"

When my daughter Reagan was six, she'd say, "Hey, Daddy. Can we play hide-and-seek?" To which I would reply, "Absolutely, baby. You hide, I'll seek." Which means I'm gonna sit here on the couch and watch some more TV until you come back, all right? But she would always go in her room, she'd hide in the same place. Then after a little while, she'd yell out, "Daddy, are you coming?"

"Honey, are you hiding?"

"Yes."

So I'd walk into her room and find her sprawled out on the floor with just her head hidden beneath the bed. "Are you in here?"

And she'd laugh, "No."

I'd drag it out a second then, "Hah, there you are. I found you."

"How did you find me?"

Well, the truth is, she was terrible at the game. Didn't really know how to hide all that well. Why? 'Cause she was six. She thought that if she couldn't see me because her head was under the bed then surely I couldn't see her.

Same thing is true here. Adam and Eve were not all that skilled at running from God. And this is what it's like when we try to run from God.

Then He asks an amazing question: "Where are you?" He knows where they are. He's not surprised. Not caught off guard. But it's an important question. You should ask yourself this right now: Where are you? More specifically, where are you in relation to Him?

Verses 10–12: And Adam said, "I heard the sound of you in the garden, and I was afraid, because I was naked, and I hid myself." And He said, "Who told you that you were naked? Have you eaten of the tree of which I commanded you not to eat?" The man said, "The woman whom you gave to be with me, she gave me fruit of the tree, and I ate." Classic man talk. "God, is it your fault or hers? I can't tell. You two get together and decide and I'll receive your apology later, all right?" Duck, cover, blame.

And so God says to the woman in verse 13, "What is this you have done?" And the woman says the same thing: *This isn't my fault.* She learned this from her husband. We know this because he's currently the only other person on planet Earth. "The serpent deceived me, and I ate." And because of that deception, sin is going to corrupt the three things that God gave to the man—the work to enjoy, the will to obey, and his woman to love.

When Adam and Eve sinned, they held the door open to all the pain and tragedy that you have ever encountered. This is why we experience bad things in this world from the macro level, like tsunamis and hurricanes, all the way to the micro level, where every cell in our bodies has been affected by the twist of sin. This is known as "the Fall."

And God said to the serpent, "Because you have done this, cursed are you above all livestock and above all beasts of the field; on your belly you shall go, and dust you shall eat all the days of your life. I will put enmity between you and the woman, and between your offspring and her offspring; he shall bruise your head, and you shall bruise his heel" (vv. 14–15). This is called the *protoevangelion*. It's the first gospel. It's the first time in scripture that we hear God speak of the rescue mission. And the rescuer.

The first thing that sin corrupts is our will to obey. And from that moment to this moment, you and I have a spiritual enemy that wants to steal, kill, and destroy us. And he whispers in your ear, "You do not have what it takes. Did God really say that?" The way this plays out, God gives us this gift of a will to obey, and then the enemy twists it either into license or legalism. The license to sin, to do what we want when we want. "I'm gonna eat the fruit, because God, I think you're withholding something from me." I'm gonna give myself a pass and call it grace.

Or, the pendulum swings to the legalism of the fig leaf where we say, "I don't need you to cover my sin. I will cover my own sin with my own self-righteousness." And that's why in here, on the inside (if you could see me, you'd see I'm tapping my chest), we begin to realize our problem is not that we sin. Our problem is that by nature and nurture, we are sinners. We are snakebit and the venom runs in all our veins. As a result, our will to obey has been corrupted. In our spirit, we want to do the right thing, what pleases God, but there is sin that dwells in us. See Romans 7. And this sin is the first curse.

We find the second curse in Genesis 3:16: "To the woman he said, 'I will surely multiply your pain in childbearing; in pain you shall bring forth children. Your desire shall be contrary to your husband, but he shall rule over you.'"

You know what this means? This means that the relationship between Adam and Eve has been damaged by sin. She who was supposed to be this perfect complement has now become a contradiction, in competition. And ladies, track with me here. You were created to help. It's just in your nature to help. And believe me, your man needs lots of help. But sometimes what you think is help feels like a hostile takeover to your husband. That word "desire" means "to take over." And instead of being a helpmate to him, you act like a dog trainer: "Come on. Come on. This is where you put that. And this is what you do here." I know you think you're helping, but you're not. This is what I mean—and I've seen this happen. You two are at a cookout and he's telling a story to his buddies. He says, "I remember. It was two years ago, Fourth of July. We were at the beach." And you interrupt him, "Actually, honey, it was six years ago, and it was Memorial Day, and we were at the lake."

In your mind you're thinking you're right and he needs correcting. You're even thinking right now, *What's wrong with that? He is so lucky to have me to point out when he gets it wrong.* And to some extent you're right. We husbands do need our wives to check us, but timing and location matter. What's more—and pay close attention to this—you are not his Holy Spirit. He needs your help, not your constant correction. Because when you do this, to him it feels like you are saying, *You are not the man, and you do not have what it takes to tell a story accurately. That is why I am here.* And this tendency in you is a result of the fall. It's like the drip-drip-drip of a leaky faucet. Which, by the way, was used as torture in previous wars. The light should be going for some of you: *Oh, my gosh. That's what's going on at home.*

The third curse as a result of the Fall is this (verse 17): "And to Adam he said, 'Because you have listened to the voice of your wife—'" Stop right there. Husbands, did you know you're not supposed to listen solely to the voice of your wife? You're supposed to listen to her heart as well, and those two things don't always line up.

Think about the last time you were driving in the car and you knew something was wrong with her, and she was looking out the window, and you said, "What's out the window?" And then twenty minutes later you figured out the problem was not outside the car, but in. And you said, "Hey, baby. What's wrong?" And she went, "Nothing." What'd you say? You said, "Good, nothing's wrong. Let's continue on with my agenda."

You listened to the voice of your wife instead of her heart, when you knew something was wrong. The Bible says that we're supposed to love our wives as unto knowledge. That means we become a student of her, and know her at the heart level, not just what she says.

Let me be clear: I'm not telling you to discount the words coming out of her mouth. Listen to those, too. But I'm also telling you to look deeper. At the heart level. Ask yourself what she's really asking or saying.

Here's a great way to get to her heart. Answer feelings with feelings and facts with facts.

Peter says in 1 Peter 3:7, "Husbands, live with your wives in an understanding way, showing honor to the woman as the weaker vessel." This means be a student of your wife.

And in Matthew 12:34, Jesus says, "Out of the abundance of the heart the mouth speaks."

If words are coming out of her mouth, they're connected to her heart. You may have to work a bit to decipher the meaning, but my point is this—don't just take the bait on the surface. Dig deeper. Listen. And then listen again.

If your wife tells you, "I just feel so fat right now," that's a feeling. Most of us hear that and immediately feel the need to communicate the solution. "Well, don't eat so much." Fact. But that's not what she needs. She needs for you to respond to her feelings with feelings of empathy and support. But anyone who has made the mistake of answering feelings with facts and who's been married for more than thirty seconds knows that's probably not the best approach. Plus, she's not asking you to fix her problem, even though that's what men are wired to do. Listen for what's being said beneath that. She might be asking, *Am I beautiful to you? Do you want to spend time with me?* Usually, there is something else bubbling beneath the surface.

Back to the third curse: "Because you have listened to the voice of your wife and have eaten of the tree of which I commanded you, 'You shall not eat of it,' cursed is the ground because of you; in pain you shall eat of it all the days of your life." God cursed the work He had given them to enjoy. Which means work is not always enjoyable, is it? "Thorns and thistles it shall bring forth for you; and you shall eat the plants of the field. By the sweat of your face you shall eat bread, till you return to the ground, for out of it you were taken; for you are dust, and to dust you shall return" (Gen. 3:18–19). And so even the work that we do was damaged by sin, and our work wars against us.

All three arenas of Adam's life are damaged by sin. The will to obey on the inside, the woman to love at home, and the work to enjoy that he goes out to do. All three were cursed. In regard to the work, the enemy comes along, takes this good gift of work from God, and then twists it. And the two extremes are either laziness or the idolatry of identifying who you are based on what you do.

So then the question becomes, "Uh, so what do we do? Do I just try harder? Man up? Cowboy up?" Nope. It won't work. It'll work till Tuesday. That's how long it'll work. And you'll probably just unleash a load of pressure on your wife and kids that they were not meant to handle.

Whenever I preach a sermon like this in our church, my phone rings the following week. It's the wife. "Listen, man. You're killing me when you do these man series, 'cause my man goes home, gets all cowboyed up, and he tries to make up for the last ten years in the next ten minutes, and it just doesn't work that way."

I know that, but the other option is guys who hear me preach and then think to themselves, *I already know I'm gonna fail, so I might as well abdicate my responsibility now.* The question for us men is what do we do, because if we man up and we try to prove our manhood by our own merit, then we end up being posers, and our wives are inherently very good at spotting a counterfeit. We think, incorrectly, that our manhood is based on things like how much money we make or what we accomplish, or how famous we are. But it's not based on that at all.

So, so here's the key. Verses 20–21: "The man called his wife's name Eve, because she was the mother of all living. And the Lord God made for Adam and for his wife garments of skins and clothed them." This is mind-blowing. Do you know what this is? This is a foreshadowing of the gospel of Jesus Christ. God looks at Adam and Eve and says, *You have sinned, and it's really bad. Much worse than you think. But your sin will be paid for, and I'm gonna make the payment. I'm gonna do for you what you could not do for you. The blood of an animal will be shed, and I will take the garments of that shed animal, and I will cover over your sin.*

Here's the point. Men, to stand up and act like a man, you must first bow down and surrender to Jesus. That's where it starts. Recognizing that we have all sinned against a Holy God and there is nothing we can do to get us back to Him. The only way we make it back to the Father is through the Grace of Jesus's blood poured out for us. To the fundamental question, "Do I have what it takes?" the absolute answer is "Absolutely not." You don't have what it takes. I don't, either. There's been only one man ever who had what it took, and He died so that we might live. But we've got to get to the place where we humble ourselves and bow, and submit our lives to the Lordship of Jesus Christ. So that the Spirit of God, the breath of life, can be breathed in you. And then and only then, with the power of Christ through the Holy Spirit living in us, can we get off our knees, stand up, and act like the men that we were called to be.

Here's the good news for anybody who is in Christ: You are more than a conqueror, and His divine power has given you everything you need to accomplish everything He's called you to do. In Christ, you have the power—through the Holy Spirit—to do whatever it is that He has called you to do. Jesus said so in John 6:63, "It is the Spirit who gives life; the flesh is no help at all."

Men, listen, I'm trying to break this down to its simplest form, to brass tacks. You have what it takes only when you bend your knee to Jesus.

Here's how I know. In Romans 5:17, the apostle Paul is talking about Adam, and he's talking about us, and he's talking about Jesus. "For if, because of [Adam's] trespass, death reigned through that one man." In other words, when Adam sinned, he infected all the sons and daughters of Adam. You know what that means? That by nature and nurture, we are sinners. We are not mistakers in need of a life coach. We are sinners in need of a savior. And Adam's sin infected the entire human experiment. "Much more will those who receive the abundance of grace and the free gift of righteousness reign in life through the one man Jesus Christ."

So Jesus Christ came to do what Adam could not do. Where Adam failed in every arena of his life, Jesus, the second Adam, lives a perfect life on our behalf. And then when he goes to the cross, He is the serpent crusher, the Lamb who was slain. And His garment was made to cover us; our sins are covered over by the righteous life of Jesus Christ.

Jesus even takes it a step further. He doesn't merely cover our sins, but according to the declaration of John the Baptist, Jesus, the Lamb of God, has come to take away our sins. Here's what that means, men: You can't do this thing on your own. You were not meant to. You will fail over and over and over. You will fail by either playing this macho role that is just silly, or you'll abdicate the responsibility that God has given you. The ultimate form of strength is to bow your knee before the almighty Jesus and say, "God, I cannot do this on my own. Please help." And that moment you surrender your life to Christ, that breath of life is breathed in you, the Spirit of God fills you, and greater is He that is in you than anything you'll face in this world. And then you get up off that mat, and you walk in a manner worthy of the gospel of Jesus Christ.

That means you are more than a conqueror. There is nothing that can separate you from God's call in your life. Neither height nor depth, neither angels nor demons, nor things in your past, nor things in your present, nor things in your future, there is no weapon formed against you that can prosper if Christ is in you.

Throughout the rest of this book, you are going to face a decision that could impact not just your life but the lives of generations after you. And it's this moment: Do you, in this moment, bow before Jesus? Honestly, did your face hit the carpet? Did you humble yourself, lay down your I-got-this mentality, and cry out to Jesus?

If you're with me on this journey, I want to ask you to stand up and act like a man. No, it's not necessary, and I know it may sound corny, and it might not be convenient, and yes, you might look foolish, but the truth is, you've probably been looking foolish your whole life and you just weren't aware. Now that you are, I am inviting you to stand up, right now, right where you are. Why? Because I want to give you this moment to submit and surrender. To be counted as a man who follows Jesus. Who has submitted to the King. And by doing so, you get to tell those around you, *I bowed before Jesus. I follow Him.*

Ladies, if you're reading this or you're aware your husband is walking through this, or maybe you saw him stand up and you thought it looked foolish, would you please reach out and take him by the hand?

Here's why: All this coming week the enemy is going to whisper in your man's ear, "You can't do this. You just got all fired up at reading a book. It'll wear off. Don't sweat it. Don't give in. You got this."

I need you to not be a nag or a drip-drip-drip, but an echo of what God wants to tell your man in his other ear: "Baby, I'm with you. I'm proud of you. And in and through Jesus, you have what it takes—to surrender and then stand and act like a man."

And if you want to throw in a "Hercules, Hercules!" just to make his chest swell, then by all means, have at it.

Men, let me pray for you.

Our good and gracious heavenly Father, Lord, I pray for the men reading this book or listening to the sound of my voice. God, I pray that we would be the prophets, the truth tellers, the priests, the caretakers of souls, the servants, the providers, and that we would take responsibility for everything that You've put under our domain. Not just provide physically, but also raise the bar and provide safe environments for the people You've put in our life so they can become who You've called them to be. God, make us the protectors You created us to be, protecting our charges not only from physical harm but from emotional and spiritual harm, too. God, please make us the men that You've called us to be, not by our own might, not by our own power, but by the spirit of the Lord. Father, I pray for resolve. I pray that from this day forward, that we would be different. That we, like Jesus, would leverage the platform that You have given us as men, to dress ourselves as servants, and to wash the feet of the people that You have put in our lives. God, I pray over these next pages and chapters that Your Holy Spirit would do the miraculous. That You would breathe life into every shell of a man reading these pages. And that at the end of the day, You will have made us men. Men who bow to You. Men who honor You. Men who bring You glory. Men who stand as prophets, providers, priests, kings, servants, and protectors. We pray this in the only name that matters. We pray this in the good, strong name of our Lord and our Savior, Jesus Christ.

DOING THE STUFF

Men, I want you to do something manly. If you're married, I want you to go find your wife, take her to a quiet place, put her in a chair or someplace where she's seated, and I want you to kneel beside her. Then take her hand and pray. Don't talk. Don't explain. Don't start a conversation. Just pray over her and for her and for your kids and your lives.

Do this out loud. Let her hear you surrender to Jesus and come under His authority and His dominion. Doesn't have to be fancy. Doesn't have to be long. And you don't have to sound eloquent. Just let her hear you humble yourself before the King.

If you're engaged, pray with your fiancée. If you're divorced, maybe a single dad, do this with your kids. If you're single, you can do this with Jesus. And, if you want to be married, you might ask Him to bring your spouse while you're there on your knees.

The point is to surrender, humble yourself before those you love, and let them watch as you bow before the King and model what it looks like to be a man of God. If you've never done it, it'll be the most manly thing you've ever done. If you're an old pro and been humbling yourself and bowing for a long time, then keep at it.

Ready, break!

Chapter 2

BE WATCHFUL

Humble yourselves, therefore, under the mighty hand of God so that at the proper time he may exalt you, casting all your anxieties on him, because he cares for you. Be sober-minded; be watchful. Your adversary the devil prowls around like a roaring lion, seeking someone to devour. Resist him, firm in your faith, knowing that the same kinds of suffering are being experienced by your brotherhood throughout the world. And after you have suffered a little while, the God of all grace, who has called you to his eternal glory in Christ, will himself restore, confirm, strengthen, and establish you.
—1 Peter 5:6–10

Toward the end of my sophomore year and the beginning of my junior year in college, I began asking what most every guy at that age asks: "What am I going to do with my life, and how am I going to make a living?"

Despite the fact that folks accuse me of sounding like a gospelized version of Larry the Cable Guy, I did really well in school. Especially in things like biology and chemistry, so I thought I'd go to medical school. I know for those of you who know me, it's comical to think that I could have actually been your doctor, but that was where I was headed. Later in my junior year, at the ripe old age of nineteen, God radically called me into the ministry. As I told you in the last chapter, when I told my daddy, he said, "Son, you don't get up and go to fun. You get up and go to work. How are you gonna do that if you only work for an hour one day a week?"

But I knew God had called me, so I made a U-turn and started visiting seminaries. My problem was that I didn't have much experience with church, and I certainly didn't know how to assess or gauge a seminary. By the way, a good starting point or litmus test for judging seminaries is to ask this: What is their belief as to the authority of the Word of God? Straight up, is every word of the Bible true or not? A good seminary believes in the authority of the Word of God, and a bad one does not.

What happened next was all my fault, and I should've done a better job, but I didn't. I chose a bad seminary. In short, they didn't believe the Bible was true, and I didn't know that until my first semester. All of the professors were very nice and polite and extremely well educated. Most of them just took a liberal posture toward the Word of God where they stood in authority over it with judgment instead of kneeling in humble submission.

The second month I was there, I attended my first New Testament class. I was pretty excited, but that excitement balloon was burst pretty quick. This was a big class and my professor was a very smart lady who'd earned her PhD in Johannine literature. Meaning, she was an expert on the Gospel of John, First, Second, and Third John, and Revelation. I was pretty fired up. But the further I got into this class, and the more I listened to her teach, I began to see that she and I held opposing views on scripture. I was what you might call a classic Christian. Orthodox in my understanding of the scripture. I believed (then and now) the Bible was true because it said it was. Period. It's either all true or none of it's true, and I believed every word was true, authored by God, and carried the authority of God. She did not.

I was soon to learn that she was a classic liberal who was making it sound like you and I could better understand all of the Bible if we did so allegorically. That the flood wasn't really a flood. That God didn't really create us. It's more of a metaphor. That the exodus of the nation of Israel from Egypt didn't occur the way it's recorded in scripture and the ten plagues were difficulties or tests to be passed. Not actual miracles. And that the miracles of Jesus could be explained away with modern science. For instance, she taught that Lazarus wasn't really dead and Mary wasn't a virgin. Stuff like that. The worst of which was she seemed to insinuate that the resurrection of Jesus was not a historical fact. That Jesus might not have physically resurrected from the grave.

Didn't take me long before I'd had about all that falsehood sandwich I could eat and I was tired of it being shoved down my throat. So, I raised my hand and called her name, and for the purpose of this I'm just going to call her Sue. So I said, "Um, Sister Sue," and she interrupted me and said, "Please don't call me sister." To which I responded, "But just last week you told us how according to the New Testament we were all brothers and sisters in the kingdom of God and that there was no hierarchy."

She didn't like that and insisted I call her professor. Directness is one of my spiritual gifts, so I said, "Professor Sue, I think when I get to heaven you're not going to be there."

She responded by saying, "That's a bold statement. Why do you say that?"

I just flat out asked her, "Do you believe in a bodily resurrection of Jesus Christ?"

To which she said, "Well, what if I don't?"

"Well, according to Romans 10:9, you will not be saved, because the Bible says that if you confess with your mouth that Jesus Christ is Lord and believe in your heart that God raised Him from the dead, you will be saved. So if you don't believe in your heart that Jesus Christ was resurrected from the grave, according to the Bible, you're not saved."

She didn't really like that, so she said, "See me after class." Which I did. And when I did, she asked me, "Why do you believe that?" Which was a really good question. At that point in my life, as a young twentysomething kid wet behind the ears, I'd never really questioned it. I'd just believed it because that was what they told me at camp. For the next eight months, I went on a deep-dive journey to learn why the resurrection was and is essential to our faith. What I came away with was a deeper conviction and deeper understanding, not only of my own personal experience with the resurrected Christ, but with the historicity of the scriptures and the overwhelming evidence of the facts and reality that there really is an empty tomb and that a once-dead Jesus really did get up and walk out of it.

I mean, for starters, if Jesus wasn't resurrected, then all the Roman soldiers had to do was roll away the stone and drag His stinking body out for all the world to see. But they didn't. Because they couldn't. Because He was alive. Walking around. Which led me to the very simple and very real realization that if the tomb is empty, then anything is possible. Including my salvation. As for my professor, I don't know if she ever believed or not. I pray she did.

Which brings me back to you. What's your relationship to the Bible? Do you believe it? Every word? Because everything I'm saying in this book is based on the fact that everything in the Bible is true. And not only true. The Bible is at least that. But it is also trustworthy. Meaning you can lean the weight of your life on it. Every promise. Everything. Period. And if you don't, if you're wishy-washy as to the facts, then your manhood will be wishy-washy, too.

You would do well to make up your mind. Because I have. And I believe every word of the Bible is true and I can place my whole trust and all my belief in it. I have, and I do. Are there parts of the Bible that are offensive and confusing and that I have a hard time understanding? For sure. The Almighty Sovereign King of the universe is its author. Even the apostle Peter confesses that the apostle Paul is a little hard to understand at times.

Yet, I believe and have experienced that the Bible is trustworthy and true. Which allows me to stand firm. You see a theme starting to rise to the surface? If you don't hold the Word of God like a rock, then your foundation is slippery. Like quicksand. But, if every word is trustworthy and true, then we can stand firm because that which we are standing firm on won't fail us. Ever.

In this chapter, we're going to look at 1 Peter 5, but before we get there, let me back up and summarize 1 Corinthians 16:13–14, which we talked about earlier. "Be watchful, stand firm in the faith, act like men, be strong. Let all that you do be done in love." Remember, I think the hub of the wheel, the core command, is to "act like men," and the imperatives around it are our marching orders on how we are to pull that off.

Easy-peazy, right?

Focus on this phrase: "Be watchful." Different translations of the Bible translate that command differently. At its root, it's a military command. Some of the other translations say, "watch out," "stand on watch," "stay alert," "be on guard." The idea here is that it's a command a commander would give a soldier to pay attention and to watch out because there is an enemy nearby. This command could be given to a soldier standing guard on a wall. It is what Jesus told His disciples to do the night He was praying in the Garden of Gethsemane. Keep watch and pray that you will not fall into temptation.

The moment I begin to think about a soldier on a wall, I think of a courtroom, Colonel Jessup on the witness stand, getting grilled by Tom Cruise. Jessup says, "Son, we live in a world that has walls, and those walls have to be guarded by men with guns. Who's gonna do it? You?... You don't want the truth because deep down in places you don't talk about at parties, you want me on that wall—you *need* me on that wall."

It paints a pretty good picture, doesn't it?

If you are a man, whether you're single, married, young, old, family, no family, whatever, being watchful is a very high calling that you were given strength to do, and not just physical strength. But here's the thing—the sum total of your strength is primarily not for you, it's for someone else. The reality of life on planet Earth is that we have an enemy, and the enemy's stated desire is to take you out. He only wants to kill, steal, and destroy you and everything and everyone that means anything to you. Why? Because if he can take out the defender, then by definition, somebody is left defenseless, making it much easier for him to accomplish his mission.

When the enemy takes one of us out, everyone suffers. The ripple effects of a man that goes down are indescribable. In fact, there's a whole lot of women and children in your orbit and mine that carry with them a great deal of pain because a man did not defend and protect. He left his post, having chosen something or someone else.

Ladies, don't think I've forgotten you. I haven't. While I'm talking primarily to men, this book can serve as a bit of a manual or an outline for what kind of man or father you should be looking for. This is not all this book is, but it's a part. I recently received a letter from a lady who attended our church, and after hearing me preach on what a Godly man is and does, she wrote this: "I just really felt compelled to thank you. I went to your church for the first time today."

Now, stop for one second. If you've ever been to our church, The Church of Eleven22, you'll hear me say all the time that it's not "my" church. It's our church. Jesus is the lead pastor, or chief shepherd, and I'm under His authority. All of us go to the same church. So if we ever meet and you attend Eleven22, then you should say, "We go to church together."

Anyway, she continued: "I sat in the back of the chairs and cried almost the whole service. Even though the sermon was about how to be a man, it struck so close to home that I knew God was talking to me through your church. See, I just recently got out of an emotionally abusive relationship. My birth father, who walked out on my mother when he found out she was pregnant, recently reconnected with me. My adoptive father was great, but I still don't know what kind of man I should be looking for. I don't know how to guard my heart. It was funny to me that the pastor said that this series may not apply to the women, but it most absolutely does. If you're single, these are the characteristics you should be looking for in a man. If you're a mother, this is what you should be teaching your daughters to look for in a husband and your sons to act like in order to become one a woman would want to have. After attending your church, my heart was overwhelmed with God's grace, God's forgiveness, and God's love, and I know it was all God's doing. But I truly needed to hear this message. I learned that I should seek a relationship with Christ first and foremost, and He will guard my heart. And I also learned the traits of the man I should give my heart to for whenever God brings him into my life. I cannot thank your church enough. I think I finally found a home after all these years of wandering."

Welcome home, I said to the lady that wrote it, *welcome home. We're glad you're here.* I don't know her whole story, but a part of the reason she endured those painful years is because some man did not do what God had created him to do on that wall that surrounded her heart. So, to all of you men, what does it mean to be watchful?

We know our enemy's stated objective because Jesus told us in John 10:10: "The thief comes *only* to steal and kill and destroy" (emphasis added). That's his mission statement. He's not your friend, not your buddy, not a fun guy to hang out with. He wants to kill you.

Need me to be more blunt? He wants to rip your head off your shoulders and post it on a stick outside the city walls. If he opens his mouth he's lying. Lying is his native tongue, and his occupation since the Garden of Eden is that of a thief and murderer. Look through the scriptures, and every time the enemy tried to thwart a great move of God, what did he do? He tried to kill all the boys, thereby taking out an entire generation of men, of upcoming guardians. Why did Moses' momma put him in the bullrushes? Because Pharaoh had commanded all the Hebrew baby boys be thrown in the Nile. And what happened when Jesus was born and Herod heard about a rival king? He killed all the boys two years and younger. And today, when I look at the world around us, it seems to me right now that the enemy is prowling around and he's trying to take out a generation of young men so that they can't rise up and be the men that God has called them to be. If our adversary can take out the defenders, then by definition those left behind will be defenseless.

So what are we watching out for? I'm glad you asked. For the answer, let's go to 1 Peter 5. In this text, Peter talks first to all the elders of the church and then to the young men. And what he gives is a strong warning. In verses 6–11: "Humble yourselves, therefore, under the mighty hand of God so that at the proper time he may exalt you, casting all your anxieties on him, because he cares for you. Be sober-minded; be watchful. Your adversary the devil prowls around like a roaring lion, seeking someone to devour. Resist him, firm in your faith, knowing that the same kinds of suffering are being experienced by your brotherhood throughout the world. And after you have suffered a little while, the God of all grace, who has called you to his eternal glory in Christ, will himself restore, confirm, strengthen, and establish you. To him be the dominion forever and ever. Amen." When the Bible says "Amen," it's not just because they couldn't think of a way to end the sentence, okay? It means "so shall it be."

This text lays out the reality that we have an enemy that wants to devour us, that wants to kill us and rip us to shreds. Not just tempt us and take us off course. But devour us. Have you ever seen a lion eat something? It's grotesque. My brother is a police officer with the St. Johns County Sheriff's Department, and sometimes, when there's roadkill, he'll go and scoop it up and carry it to this big cat zoo thing in St. Augustine, where they've got this lion named Mufasa. One time, my brother tosses a deer over the fence into the lion cage. Meanwhile, Mufasa is just lying there staring at all the people that are staring at him. When the deer lands with a thud, Mufasa stands up, stretches, and meanders over. Then he leans down, without taking his eye off all the people, and grabs that little doe by the head like he's picking up a peanut M&M. Then, with a single twitch, he snaps its head off. You don't jack around with a lion, right?

In the text, I see at least four tactics—four ways that men typically are taken out by this enemy—and we're going to look at each of them in this chapter. Then I'm going to throw a fifth one in there for free. The fifth one is a little bit of a stretch because it's not in the text, but there's no way I could talk about the enemy taking out men without talking about this one.

The first one is addressed by this command: "Humble yourselves, therefore, under the mighty hand of God so that at the proper time he may exalt you." Number one is pride. Can I get a witness? Anybody wrestle with that one?

One of the big ways, if not the biggest way, that the enemy tries to take us men down is pride. Pride is simply when we think too much of ourselves and too little of others. When we compare ourselves to other people. Most of this occurs in silent conversations that no one else can hear. This is called the sin of comparison, and nothing feeds it more than social media. Pride is that feeling you get when you walk into Walmart late at night and look around at who else is there. When you compare yourself to who else is there, you start feeling pretty good about yourself. Justifying yourself. It's just true. If you want to existentially experience the grace of God in John 3:16, "For God so loved the world," go to Walmart at 1:00 p.m. on a Christmas Eve.

Every single one of us will scratch our heads and ask ourselves, "He loves all these people?"

And the answer is "Absolutely, yes."

And here's the truth: He loves them just as much as He loves you. No difference. Our pride bubbles up when we compare ourselves to others and we just think we're better. Pride is when we think the world is about us and you ask, "Why me, God?" Pride is when, in your heart of hearts, you think the earth revolves around you. That it's His job to make you happy.

Here's the thing about pride. Almost no one admits to it. We all think pride is someone else's problem. I've been in ministry for thirty-one years, and I have never had one person come and sit down in my office and say, "Well, Pastor, let me tell you what my problem is. I'm just prideful." Not one person. Why? Because it's so easy to see in everybody else, and it's so hard to see in ourselves.

C. S. Lewis says that pride is the greatest of all sin. The reality is this: The Bible says that God opposes the proud. Think about that. It's totally contrary to the message of the world. That means when you're prideful, God stands in front of you. Opposing you. When in all of human history did that turn out good for anyone? You want that? If you want God to be on the other side of you, preventing you from doing whatever it is that you've got your mind set on, then be proud.

Prideful people have two options: Be humbled or be humbled. That's it. Every knee will bow before the name of Jesus. So you can either bow now at a time of your choosing or wait until it's too late and bow at a time of His choosing.

I've heard some people say, "I'll tell you what, man, when I see Jesus, I'ma ask Him." Stop. You ain't asking jack. You're gonna lay on your face like a dead man and pray like crazy He doesn't zap you with a lightning bolt... that's what's happening.

One of the key questions I get from people that have known me for a long time is, "How do you keep from being so prideful with everything that's going on at Eleven22?" It's a legit question, I understand. We have a lot going on at our church and it'd be really easy to listen to the whisper of the enemy and start taking credit for it, but here's the thing—this movement is exponentially bigger than anything that I could dream up or imagine. I didn't do this. He did. Still is. If you read my last book, *Run Over by the Grace Train*, you've heard me say that when a mosquito latches hold of a freight train, he does not feel bigger. He holds on for dear life. I'd like to think that's me. By the grace of God, I'm holding on and praying to remain faithful.

The reality is we all struggle with pride. So, let me ask you this: Are you prideful? The answer is yes, because you're human, but let me help you pinpoint it. Ask yourself a few questions: Do you seek credit? When you're at work and they're talking about a division that overperformed, are you just waiting on your name to be called? Do you have a problem complimenting others? Especially when you know you were responsible for the good job? Here's one: Are you put off when you don't get a thank-you? You know why I put that one? Because that's me. My love language is gratitude, and when people don't express it, I can get grumpy. And this is not like Jesus.

If you've been around me or my teaching for more than five minutes, you know that I write sermons and books in the woods. It's where I think best. And normally, it's where I'm comfortable. But as I wrote this particular chapter, I started getting a little fidgety. This one struck a little too close to home. The problem with this particular part of this chapter is that the Lord peeled back the layers and let these words start preaching to me. Which is dangerous. This might be a really long chapter. While writing this, I took a look in the mirror, and it didn't take me long to realize, *Uh-oh. I'm talking to me. About me. I'm pretty sure I have a pride issue. Maybe I need people to say "thank you" to me because I think I had something to do with the success of this church.*

How about this one: When people scroll through your Facebook, X, and Instagram accounts, what do they say? What's the message you're sending? Because you have one. Does your message say how great you are or how great God is? Is your social media all about you and your wonderful life?

Let's look deeper. This might even be worse. Have you crafted a passive-aggressive social media message about how great your God is when, in reality, it's really all about you? Wanting people to know what a righteous Christian you are? Oh, am I getting too close to home? Did that one sting?

Moving down the line, do you always have to be right? Honest confession, this is also me. Writing this has been like therapy. I know a lot of Bible verses and when someone wants to argue with me I'm like, "Bring it on." Truth is, I just have a pride problem.

Given that this is our universal problem, what do we do? Well, for starters, we humble ourselves under the mighty hand of God. One of the key ways to fight pride in your life is to worship. Find a gospel-centered church, sit under the teaching of the Word of God, and when you come before the Lord, don't pretend it's Christian karaoke. It's not. In my church, we sing our faces off. Hands up. Top of our lungs. Why? Because we can. Because the God of the universe actually took the time to think us up. Because He loves us with a depth of love none of us can imagine. And because He did for me, for you, for all of us, what none of us could do in ten thousand lifetimes. Jesus paid our debt. Died in our place. Satisfied the wrath of God. Returned us to the Father.

Imagine you're in a court of law. On trial for murder. The judge slams the gavel, declares you guilty, and sentences you to death by hanging. And as you're walking to the gallows, I stand in front of you and take your place. You go free, while they throw the little lever and the rope snaps my neck. What would you do? For starters, you'd probably name your kids after me. Jesus' offer is ten thousand times greater. He offers to free you from eternal damnation. From eternal separation from the Father. And to return you—not as a slave but as an heir, with all the rights and privileges of a son or daughter—to the Father.

When we worship, when we magnify the name of God, two things simultaneously happen. One is we grow increasingly aware of our utter depravity and understand that we cannot depend on ourselves. When we make more of Him, we realize how unworthy we are in comparison. Simultaneous to that, we grow in our understanding of the magnificence and omnipotence of God. We begin to understand how truly awesome He is and how much we are not.

When I look out across our church, I see that generally the women worship much more than the men. They're more expressive. Most men stand there with their hands in their pockets. Transport them to an NFL game and put beer in their hands, and they're jumping up and down and raising both hands and screaming at the top of their lungs when their gridiron hero carries the little pigskin across a painted line. But put them in church before the God of this universe and every other, who spoke everything we see in existence and who offers every one of us a return to the Father, and at best we're indifferent. Our response is to shrug and say, "Eh."

Why do we do this? Because we're deeply prideful. We're too prideful to open our mouths to the one that opened His mouth and created everything. We're too prideful to lift our hands to the one who stretched out His hands and died for us and in our place because we think we're tough or too cool to show emotion. You do know that Paul tells Timothy that *men* should lift holy hands in the sanctuary, right? Not showing emotion is not tough. It's stupid. So is not worshipping. You want to see a tough man, watch the men in the front row, hands in the air, veins popping out on their necks 'cause they're singing so loud. Because in that moment, they have humbled themselves before the Almighty God.

Not only that, worship is warfare. Satan was kicked out of heaven because he was tired of being looked through as an angel of light. He was in charge of leading the angelic host in worshipping the one true God, but he wanted to be looked to. That is pride. Satan's desire was to sit on the throne of heaven that is reserved for God alone. Satan's plan was to overthrow the King of Kings so that he would be worshipped. Every time we join our voices together with the saints and declare God Almighty is worthy of our worship, then we are simultaneously putting the devil of hell in his place and reminding him that he is not. Real men worship.

Toward the end of the Book of Job, Job puts God on trial. "God, why did you let this happen to me?" And then God replies to Job. You should read it for yourself. The last five chapters of the Book of Job, God replies to Job. He tells him to dress himself like a man and get ready for this. And then He begins to interrogate Job.

He starts off with this: "Where were you when I laid the foundation of the earth?" (Job 38:4).

How do you answer that? In short, He's asking, *"When I was deciding how many planets there would be...I don't remember you helping me. And do you know where I keep the snow? Do you know where it's gonna lightning next?"*

Basically, what He's saying is, *"Job, there are parts of your back you can't even scratch. Who are you to even come and question me, the Almighty Sovereign God? I mean, really, do you think you have things under control? You can't even lick your own elbow."*

Here's the thing. Humility is not a feeling. Humility is a posture. A response to God. A response born out of knowing who He is and who we are in light of Him. Humility is like exercise; it's a thing we do. An action. We posture ourselves before the Lord and bow. Knee to the dirt. Face to the carpet. And when we do, the Bible tells us that He will lift us up, exalt us, in His time. And when He does, you won't have to apologize in some sort of false humility. Never apologize for the Lord's anointing. Just walk in it. But when He does lift you up, watch out for pride. And humble yourself again. How? Bend the knee, throw your hands in the air, sing at the top of your lungs, and worship. Don't compare yourself to everybody else. Compare yourself to almighty God and watch what happens. You will be humbled.

Some of you need to hear this—if you're struggling with sin, any sin, and especially pride, drag it into the light. Confess it. If you try and fight the enemy in the dark, he'll kick your tail. Period. You don't stand a chance. This is why John, the brother of Jesus, said, "But if we walk in the light, as he is in the light, we have fellowship with one another, and the blood of Jesus his Son cleanses us from all sin" (John 1:7).

Back to 1 Peter 5. The enemy's second weapon is revealed in verse 7: "Casting all your anxieties on him, because he cares for you." There it is in black-and-white—anxiety. What the Bible calls "anxiety" we tend to call "worry." Now watch the progression. First up is pride, followed closely by worry and anxiety. It's like clockwork. Most often, men worry about work and money. Or, at least that's what they say they're worried about. Truth is, their identity is wrapped up in both so, in their pride, they begin to "worry" about what'll happen to their identity if they experience a change in either their title at work or the amount of money they make.

The reality is that God gives us this incredible gift, work to enjoy, along with the command to subdue and cultivate, so that we could be cocreators with Him in this incredible thing that He's given us called the earth. He actually calls us to rearrange the raw materials of this earth for human flourishing. For His glory. And then the enemy comes along and twists it, and what was once a work to enjoy becomes an idol in our life where we begin to find our identity in our activity.

When people ask you, "What do you do for a living?" we assume they mean our vocation. And wanting to sound like we have our stuff together, because we're afraid to let people know the truth, which is that we don't, we work really hard so our answer sounds good. So it makes us sound important. Like a boss. A man on the move. #crushinit. And there are a lot of you reading this right now who are killing yourselves in jobs you don't love. You haven't spent a weekend with your wife and kids in months because you've made your work and the identity that results from it an idol. That's right.

The enemy is a master at taking a good thing like work to enjoy and that provides for your family and twisting it to become the source of your identity, when your identity should be the one that gave you the job to begin with. Not only that, but you're hiding behind your work. Masking your own insecurity with lies like "Yeah, I'm just trying to provide for my family." Baloney. You want to look good in other people's eyes, and you think your vocation does that for you. It's why you dress the way you do. To display your power. How you've got it all together.

When was the last time you asked your family what they wanted? Because I can promise you this: They want you more than the stuff that you can provide. That's just true. I don't know any kids that are real proud of or care that much at all about the house they live in. And given the choice between long hours in it without you or long hours with you and a smaller house, they'll take you. What's worse, we blame our idolatry on the people we love the most. Meaning, we tell them they're the reason we're doing all this. Wrong. They're not. If you think I'm poking you in the chest, let me let you in on a secret. So far in this little rundown of the enemy's weapons and how he uses them against us, I'm batting 0 for 2 right now. I'm not enjoying this any more than you are.

Ladies, let me let you in on a secret. We men don't necessarily care if we're liked. At some level we do, but at the end of the day, we just want to be impressive—to other people. Hated or loved, it doesn't matter, just not ignored. To combat this, we drive stuff we often can't afford and convince ourselves we like it to impress people we don't even know. So back to you men. Some of whom are now squirming in your seats. Let me ask you: Are you worried? Anxious? Let me ask it this way: If God is who He says He is, and He loves you like scripture says He loves you, what do you really have to be worried about? I mean, really? Now, look at all the stuff you worry about. Spread it out across the table in front of you. What can you really do about it? Truth is, it's not the work you're worried about. It's not really the job. It's how you can look better than someone else doing the same job, which is the comparison game, which is rooted in your pride. See how this works?

There is a fine line between concern for the welfare of your family and the idolatry and envy that comes when you try to control the situation out of fear. I would ask it this way—are you putting your faith in your circumstances or in your sovereign Savior? Are you putting your faith in your job, in your health, in your relationships? Is that where your faith is? Or are you putting your faith in your sovereign Savior? If you stripped all of those things away, would He still be enough? I'm not saying it wouldn't hurt like crazy, but would He still be enough?

Do you see how the enemy can take us out with worry and anxiety? So what do you do? Let's go back to 1 Peter 5:7. "Casting all your anxieties on him, because he cares for you." I lead a disciple group of men. You'd think that because I'm the pastor that I help them, but truth is, they help me. They help me a lot. There's a guy in my group named Luke, and he unpacked what this *cast all your cares on Him* is all about. He said, "When it says 'cast,' it means 'to throw away or cast off,' like you would take your cares and you would chuck them. But I think a lot of us cast our cares on Jesus like you cast a rod and reel. You're saying, 'Here we go, I'm gonna cast it on Him.' Problem is, you're still holding on to one end. Why? So you can reel it back in." He's right. We do. Why? Because, at the end of the day, we don't trust Him, so we think we have to control it. Tell me I'm lying.

At the end of every service, I say to our church, "We respond in three ways, and one of the ways is to come down here and you bend your knee to Jesus. Cast your cares upon Him because He cares for you. Come and pray." And you know what a lot of us do? We kneel down and cast our cares upon Him, but at the end of our prayer we just reel that thing in and take it right back to our seat. The command from Peter is to sling that thing on Jesus. Let it go. Let it pass out of your hands and into His. I don't know about the worries and the cares in your life, but I know I can walk up to the altar, drop my cares, and leave them right there in a huge steaming pile—but without fail, they somehow find me while I'm sleeping and crawl back into my brain. That's why the ESV says, "casting." It's not a onetime event. It's a daily event.

One of the first senior pastors that I worked for, Dr. Bill Ross, said this: "If you pray, why worry? And if you worry, why pray?" Worry is the antiprayer. So what do you do when you're paralyzed by worry? Cast your cares upon Him. Why? Because He cares for you. Even if you think your deal is not that big a deal. Don't ever compare your pain or anxiety to anybody else's. He's a good dad. He loves you. And if it's important to you, it's important to Him.

How do I know this? When my kids were young, they'd bring home art projects on Sunday from our kids' ministry. And let's be honest. They were not all that great. I never told them that, but da Vinci or stick drawing didn't matter. What mattered is that they brought them to me. Climbed up in my lap. Wanted me to see them. Wanted me to tape them to the refrigerator door. "Daddy, are you proud?" To which I answered, "Yes." Because I was then and am now. Why? Because they're some great artist? No. Because they're my kids and I love them with a love they won't understand until they have kids of their own. It's just the way it works. My love for them is not dependent upon the quality of their artwork. In reality, it doesn't depend on anything. It just is. And always will be. Period. Same with Jesus, except on an exponentially greater level. So you bring all your junk to Jesus. It matters to Him because you matter to Him.

The third thing that the enemy uses is found in verse 8: "Be sober-minded; be watchful." Laziness and abdication of responsibility is a straight-up tool of the enemy. "Sober-minded" means "stays alert." "Be watchful" literally means, "Wake up." Some of you are literally and figuratively just sitting on the couch drinking beer and eating potato chips while the whole world is passing you by. The enemy is coming after your family, and some of you literally need to sober up. Truth is, you can't address the minded part until you get sober. Only then can you retake your place on the wall and be watchful.

Some of you aren't wrestling the addiction demon; you've cozied up with the laziness demon and you need to get off your blessed assurance and get in the game. Fact is, you're just lazy. Straight up. Let me let you in on a secret. There is a part of the American dream that is 100 percent at odds with the message of the gospel. The pursuit of comfort. Nowhere in scripture does it say to pursue it or that God owes it to you. If you wanna pursue a comfortable life, then do not follow Jesus. Just don't.

This is not a trick question—do you know what it means to be a follower? It means you follow somebody. You go where they go. Where did Jesus go? To the cross. Everybody wanted to follow Him after He fed the five thousand, or walked on water, or healed the man born blind or the paralytic, or called Lazarus out of the tomb, but the moment He strapped that cross bar to His shoulders, nobody followed Him. They all abandoned Him. Why? Because He was walking to His death. So, you should just know that when Jesus says, "Follow me," He is saying, *"Come and die with me."*

Does that sound like the comfortable life? No. The comfortable life is at odds with the gospel. So be very careful that you do not seek comfort, because He has called us to lay down our lives. Are you lazy? Are you pursuing the comfortable life? Are you just sitting on the couch covered in cheese puffs and empty beer cans? If you are bored in your life and Jesus is your Lord, I've got some news for you: There's this thing called the Great Commission. We're supposed to take the gospel into the four corners of the earth. So, here, let me fill up the rest of your calendar. Go take the gospel to the hardest, most unsavable person you can think of.

Get out there. Share the gospel. If that's not enough, there are a lot of unreached people groups who've never heard the gospel. Pack up and go. Move there. You won't be bored. Jesus said, *"Love the Lord your God with all your heart, soul, mind, and strength, and love your neighbor as yourself"* (Mark 12:30–31). Show me someone doing this and I'll show you someone who is not lazy, and not bored. They wake up every single day with something to do. It doesn't take a genius to know that one of our biggest problems as a society is our insatiable desire for comfort and for the artificial manipulating of our own image. Don't think so? Then explain Botox, Spanx, and most plastic surgery. Here's the truth of us: We're getting older. Age is catching up. Nobody gets to outrun it. Get over yourself. It's gonna happen.

Truth is, you know who notices us the most? We do. We look at ourselves all the time, and because we do, we think other people do, too. But you know who doesn't notice themselves or other people's wrinkles? People that are getting after the mission of God, because they don't have time for that kind of stuff.

So, let me poke at you a little bit more. Are you lazy? Do you need to wake up? Ask yourself this: What are the distractions in your life? Are you more consumed with your hobby than your calling? And, for the record, your calling is your family and your mission. Are you more concerned with your fantasy football team or your handicap than you are the people in your home? Are you more concerned with your hunting season than this season in life that God has given you? Laziness is more than not doing something. It's also avoiding something. What hard conversation, what hard decision, what hard action do you know God is calling you to, and you're just avoiding it by being lazy?

God would say to you, "Be sober-minded and be watchful." Wake up and get after it. How? Just start with one step. Wake up, get your mind right, and do something in the kingdom of God for the kingdom of God. Need some suggestions? Men, pursue your wife. When was the last time you dated your wife? Like you did back before you were married, back when you actually made a reservation and planned a date? I know you can, because you convinced her to marry you. Truth is, most of us outpunted our coverage. But back when you had game, what did you do? You weren't lazy then. She never would have married you if you were. You pursued. You called. Bought flowers. Watched dumb movies and cried at all the right times. You walked on the beach and you don't even like the beach. You ate frozen yogurt and you don't even like it. Study your wife, and see what happens. You've gotten lazy, so get back in the game, and pursue your wife.

Next, pursue the hearts of your children. I'm convinced most parents are far more concerned about where their kids are going to college than where they're going to spend eternity. If that stings a little, it's probably true. Do you spend more time on homework than the Word of God? Here's a simple remedy—get you a *Jesus Storybook Bible* and just start reading it with them. Out loud. The crazy thing is, you'll learn a lot about the scriptures, too. I fail in this so many times. Why? Because in the midst of all that we have going on in our grown-up worlds, it's hard to sit with our kids long enough to get into theirs.

Gretchen and I laugh about other peoples' perception of me and my family. It is comical. Most folks think that because I'm a pastor, when I get home, I just fold my hands and say, "Kids, gather around.

It is family devotion time," and to start things off, Gretchen breaks out into a worship song. Then, because we've trained them so well, my kids sit down with their own Bibles and highlighter pens and say, "Oh father, please teach us the word of God."

Nothing could be further from the truth. My house, like your house, is a train wreck. My kids fuss and fight. When JP was younger, he was into dragons and *The Lord of the Rings*, so every time we sat down to do any sort of family devotion he would say, "Dad, do the one about the dragon at the end." To which Reagan would respond, "A dragon? Dad, I'm scared." And then run to her room where she'd get on the phone with her friends. When I would look to Gretchen for a little help, she'd be scrolling through Pinterest. Then to top it off, I'd have to spend the next several hours apologizing for my anger. Total train wreck. A lot of times, we just punt.

Husbands, let me speak directly to you a minute. Do you pray for and with your wives? There's a reason I ended the last chapter the way I did. It wasn't just a gimmick to fill space on the page. So, do you? When I've asked this to guys, some of the responses I get sound like, "Oh, pastor. I'm not a good prayer. Biggest word I know is 'delicatessen' and I don't know how to work it into the prayer."

Let me let you in on a little secret. Your wife doesn't care. Hold her hand, and then say, "Baby, how can I pray for you?" She is then going to open her mouth and say stuff. Now, this is important. Pay attention. Pay attention to the exact words she says. Remember them. This would be a good time to be alert. Sober-minded. Then when she's finished, you bow your head, close your eyes, and you say, "Dear God...," and then you just say the stuff she just said. Just repeat it back to the Lord. Don't get fancy. Don't call an audible. Just say what she said. Be sober-minded. Be watchful. Then when you're finished, say, "Amen." And when you get done, she's going to be crying. And you're going to want to ask her, "What's wrong?" but don't do that. Nothing's wrong. For maybe the first time in a long time, everything's right. So get in the game. Pray for your wife.

Now look at the second half of verse 8: "Your adversary the devil prowls around like a roaring lion, seeking someone to devour." The enemy's fourth tactic is isolation. Men are expert isolationists. You know why? Because we think, *I got this*. Guess what, bro? You ain't got this. You were created in the image of God, and God said it is not good that man be alone. That didn't just mean Adam needed a date. God Himself is in a relationship. How? God the Father, God the Son, God the Holy Spirit. The Godhead is a plurality—one God, three persons—and if you think you can do this on your own, you are not imaging God whatsoever. If in the Garden of Gethsemane, Jesus asked for His disciples to watch and pray with Him, then who do you think you are to think you can live this life on your own? Let me repeat: You don't got this. So, don't pound your chest and tell yourself that you do. You don't. Never have.

Think about it this way. In prison, the ultimate form of human punishment is isolation. You've seen enough animal shows to know this. Who does the lion attack? It's always that one stray on the edge. Bringing up the back of the pack. Why? Because the lion will get trampled if he tries to get to the middle. Doesn't stand a chance. Too many hooves. Too many horns. The reason the herd exists is to surround the weak ones, the ones that are hurt, the ones that are stumbling, the ones that have fallen, the ones that are bleeding, and the ones that need the help. All the infirm go to the middle while the strong ones create the hedge to prevent the lion from taking out the weak ones. Which should be a beautiful picture of the church.

Except it's not. We as a church have failed miserably at this. More often than not, the church ostracizes the weak, wounded, and infirm. And if that's you, if you were weak, infirm, broken, needing triage, and you went to a church and they put you on the outside or didn't gather around you and get you the healing you needed, please hear me, don't let the abuses or the wounding of other broken people keep you from the love of Jesus. Please don't reject Jesus because you have had a bad experience with religious people. Jesus, on almost every page of the four gospels, had bad experiences with religious people. Please come back. The enemy will use other people's brokenness to wound you and then devour you. Please, walk in forgiveness. Come back to the herd. Get in the middle. To the rest of you, if you're in a season of strength in your walk with Jesus, then walk to the edge and grab one of the weak, who are struggling, who don't think they fit in, and say, "Come on. Come with me. Get in here in the middle." That's church.

The lion always picks off the strays, so let me ask you, men, are you isolated? Some of you say, "No, man, I'm not isolated. I have six hundred friends on Facebook." News flash—those are not your friends. Let me ask you this. Who's praying for you specifically, right now? Who, this week, have you shared the hard stuff with? Have you said, "Hey man, I need you to pray with me" about what's concerning you? Who really knows how you're doing and what you're doing?

If your life blows up, who are you going to call? A band of brothers is like a retirement account. If you wait until you need it to build it, it's over. It's too late. You've got to build that thing now before you need it because when you do, it'll be too late. Most guys pound their chests, say, "I got this," and think, *Well, I'll just call on Jesus.* The three most dangerous words a man can ever say are, "I got this." There was only one man in the history of men who had it, and you're not Him. All the rest of us don't got it. That's why we need the One who did and still does. And in His mercy, He gave you brothers to walk with and alongside. So, who do you have in your life?

Mark 2 records that there was a paralyzed man who needed help. He had four friends each grab a corner of his mat and carry him to

Jesus. I wrote about this in *Anything Is Possible*. Can you write down four names of mat carriers who would do what it takes to get you to Jesus in your time of need?

If your honest answer is, "Well, I don't have those kinds of men in my life. I'm kinda isolated. What do I do?" then you've asked a great question. And it's a great place to start. First, join a disciple group. A Bible study. A small group. Which assumes you're in a church. And eighteen holes on a Sunday morning is not a church. I've met guys who cringe at joining a disciple group: "Yeah, but I don't know the Bible." That's like saying, *I'm out of shape. I can't go to the gym.* Are you really being serious? Go. Get plugged in. You'll be in good company with people just like you, and you will be amazed at how few people know the Bible.

There will be one guy, he knows the Bible super well. He's usually self-righteous. A bit of a Pharisee. He's the prideful one. Here's the thing: He needs to be there, just like you. Maybe more. The two of you can learn to walk together. Get plugged in.

The fifth tactic of the enemy is not explicitly stated in the text, but I think we, as men, can all admit it's in there. Say this out loud with me. This is verse 9: "Resist him, firm in your faith, knowing that the same kinds of suffering are being experienced by your brotherhood throughout the world." The enemy uses pride, worry, laziness, and isolation, and he uses one more, and it might be the most powerful weapon he has. While all of these are arrows in his quiver, it's like he dips this one in gasoline and sets it on fire. This last one is lust. And believe me, "the same kinds of suffering are being experienced by your brotherhood throughout the world."

How many men have blown up their entire lives, families, kids, and careers all because of lust? You see where it says, "Resist him, firm in your faith." That is true. We are to resist the enemy and stand firm in faith, except in one area. When it comes to lust, you're supposed to run. Flee. Turn, and hightail it. The Bible commands us in many places, but 1 Corinthians 6:18 is the clearest. It says, "Flee from sexual immorality." That means "Run away." Most of the time we flirt with it. We like to see how close we can go to the line and not cross it, and then once we do we just simply move the line and justify that it was in the wrong place to begin with. Or, even if we know we are crossing the line into sin we then ask, "Well, how far over the line can I go and still manage the consequences?"

Let me put it this way: If you were walking through a parking lot, on the way to your car, and the devil himself was sitting in your car, then you put on the full armor of God and tell him to get out of your car. That's not his car. That's Jesus' car. He doesn't belong in there. You put on the helmet of salvation and the breastplate of righteousness and the belt of truth and have your feet fitted with the gospel of readiness of peace, then take up the shield of faith and the Word of God and you kick some devil tail. Do your thing. "Get out of my car, devil! Greater is He that is in me than that snake that is in my car."

But if, on the way home, you find your ex-girlfriend parked in your driveway, you keep on going. Mash the gas pedal. Don't pass Go. Don't collect two hundred dollars. Just get.

Men, we are to flee sexual immorality. Not flirt with, not dance around the edges, not justify and compromise, not play stupid, not dabble with. You and I are to flee. Period. The question is, are you fleeing or flirting? In my opinion, this is the granddaddy of them all.

I was on a men's retreat one time, and we were studying the Book of Genesis. I asked a question: "Why do you think God put the tree of the knowledge of good and evil in the garden?" One of the guys responded, "It's easy to do what's right if right is the only option." Think about that. It's easy to do what's right if right is the only option. Men, let me help you here. Make your wife the only option. Decide that she is and always will be the only option. Rules don't make man righteous, but rules can help keep you out of trouble, so put rules around your rules. Don't travel alone. Don't ride alone with another woman who's not your wife. Don't meet in your office with a woman not your wife with the door closed. Don't put yourself in places where darkness can cause the appearance of evil. And when it comes to apps on your phone, delete them all. Starting with TikTok. I don't care what people think about you; these apps are designed as clickbait, and sooner or later they will catch you with your guard down. Does your wife know the code to your phone? Does she have the right to peruse your phone at any time? Why not? Don't you want her to? What do you have to hide? We have an enemy that prowls around like a roaring lion and he does not want you married, he does not want you faithful; he wants you prideful, worried, lazy, isolated, lustful, and not fleeing. Because then you're a dead man.

Are you fleeing or flirting? Start thinking about it this way. That girl at work with the sweet laugh who's just a friend who "gets you" and thinks you're funny? Maybe she lingers a little too long after a meeting. Great listener. Longing eyes. She's a lioness that wants to kill you. She's a temptress from hell. You can tell her I said so. "Sorry, Pastor Joby said you were trying to kill me." The moment you think, *Oh, it's a harmless activity*, it's not. It is a tool in the hand of the enemy, and he is trying to devour you. Kill, steal, and destroy you and your life. So what do you do? You flee.

Ask yourself this: If you were your enemy, how would you come after you? The answer is where you need to fight. The place where you're most likely to fall is the place where you need to get in the game and fight. But don't fight alone. And men, the answer to your problem, the help that you need, is not found in you. You don't got it. Without Jesus and His Spirit living inside you, you won't be able to "cowboy up" and you won't be able to "try harder." The answer that you need, the solution, is found in the God-man who does for us what we cannot do for ourselves.

That's why verse 10 begins, "And after you have suffered a little while..." You know what this means. It means this is a fight. And in a fight, you get punched. Which means that if you're not getting knocked around a little bit, if you're not getting punched, you might not be in the fight. Because the enemy is not coming after you. I know this sounds mean, but I love you enough to be mean to you. The reason he might not be your enemy is because you've joined his team. You're helping him out. If you don't feel the incredible current of our culture pushing against you, maybe it's because you're just in the current. You're like that turtle in the Nemo movie riding the Gulf Stream. If you wake up every morning and you've got a bloody nose because the enemy is punching you, congratulations. Welcome to the battle. So, men, fight, fight, fight.

First Peter 5:10 says, "And after you have suffered a little while, the God of all grace..." Do you know why He's called "the God of all grace"? Because when you stand up and try to act like a man, and then stumble and fall on your face, you fall on grace. That's what you fall on. You fall into the arms of our heavenly Father, who picks you up again and stands you on your feet and says, "Look, I put you on this wall. I want you here. With my power living in you, you can accomplish all that I have called you to. I'm with you. I'll never leave you." Then He says this: "...who has called you to his eternal glory in Christ, will himself restore, confirm, strengthen, and establish you." This means Jesus Himself will do in you what you've been trying to do on your own.

Don't miss those four words: "restore," "confirm," "strengthen," "establish." He will restore. If you've fallen short in what it means to be a man, if there are people drowning in your wake—maybe an ex, or kids that you don't see—and you feel like there's a whole season of your life that you missed out on by your own doing, well, I've got great news. He is a restorer, and He can restore what the locusts have eaten. He Himself will restore and confirm. God always confirms what He calls, and if He called you to be a man, He will confirm it. The way He most often confirms it is not from some kind of majestic voice out of heaven. He often confirms it in the friendships, in the brotherhood of the people that He puts around you.

When I began to walk closely with some brothers and really open up and share my junk, here's what began to happen. They began to see in me things that I never saw in me. Coach Bull Lee, the guy that led me to the Lord, did the same thing. One summer, when I was nineteen and serving at a church camp, he volun-told me to preach my very first sermon.

"But Coach, I don't feel comfortable talking in front of people."

He looked at me like I'd lost my mind. "Boy, did you say 'comfortable'? Boy, do you think Daniel was comfortable in the lions' den? Boy, do you think Paul and Silas were comfortable in the prison? Boy, do you think Jesus was comfortable on the cross?"

He had a point, but that didn't solve my next problem. "Well, what do I talk about?"

"You talk about Jesus, and you talk about thirty minutes."

So I did. Albeit reluctantly. I walked up onstage and unpacked John 3:16. Why? Because I knew where to find it in the Bible. The sermon was terrible but God used it, as He often does, and a few kids got saved. When I walked off of the tiny stage, Coach Bull put his finger in my chest and barked, "Boy, when you teach the Bible I see two things happen. I see you come alive. And I see them come alive."

Last time. First Peter 5:10. "And after you have suffered a little while, the God of all grace, who has called you to his eternal glory in Christ, will himself restore, confirm, strengthen, and establish you." Restore and confirm and strengthen and establish. Some of you brothers have been fighting the good fight and you're tired. Worn down. Got the battle scars to prove it. I've got good news for you. That by the power of the Holy Spirit, He will strengthen those who wait upon the Lord. Count on the strength of the Holy Spirit and He will restore, confirm, strengthen, and establish you. This means that if you've been knocked off the wall, Jesus comes along and restores you, confirms you, strengthens you, and establishes you by putting you back on that wall.

Here's the point. The rebellious person gives in to the temptation of the forbidden fruit, follows their own desires, and ends up, despite some fun along the way, being devoured. Lion food, which just becomes lion poop. The religious person gives in to the temptation of the fig leaf, thinking that by the works of their own hands they can cover over their sin and shame and therefore don't need God. They follow their own rules and they end up, despite great effort, being devoured. Also lion food and lion poop.

But the gospel-centered person follows Christ. Regardless of what you've done, regardless of your past, regardless of what has been taken from you, regardless of how many times the enemy has defeated you, if you are in Christ, then you are fighting from victory and not for victory. So let me bring it full circle: Humble yourself and cast all your cares upon Him because He cares for you. Be sober-minded and watch out.

Bottom line, be watchful. Get in the game. Be ready to both attack the enemy and flee sexual immorality. Don't get sucked in. And in order to do this, you've got to have your eyes peeled to the spiritual reality around you. God has great things in store for you, so humble yourself under the mighty hand of God and He may, at the right time, exalt you.

PRAY WITH ME

Our good and gracious heavenly Father, I thank You that You are a good dad and You love Your kids. And Father, I thank You so much for these men reading these pages. Lord, I pray that we would be watchful and that You would establish us on that wall. I pray, whether we're married or single, whether we've got kids or grandkids or no kids, whether we're teenagers or old guys, that we would be watchful and that we would act like men. Father, please help us leverage whatever You have given us for Your glory and, in so doing, for our joy. Father, I pray against pride. And I pray against laziness. And against isolation. And Lord, I pray against lust and sexual immorality and any other weapon that the enemy tries to form against us. We know that it cannot and will not prosper because when Christ was on the cross, he said, "It is finished." That means You win, and because You win, we win. So Lord, I pray that You would strengthen these men by the power of the Holy Spirit and that starting now, the children and wives and coworkers and bosses and friends would be blessed because these men would lead and love well. We pray this in the name of Jesus. Amen.

DOING THE STUFF

Your job this week is to find four brothers you can pray with and share embarrassing stuff with, and who will shoot straight with you and not judge you. These are four men who love Jesus and love their families. Remember the old adage: Show me your friends and I'll show you your future. So, find four men who will humble themselves and bow the knee to Jesus, and then you all stand up together. Maybe you all should read this book together. And if you don't have four friends you can call, then either you need to find a church or you need to find a new church. Because real men love Jesus and they go to church. And the best way to find these four men is to commit to be that kind of man for others. God loves to answer the prayer of the man who is asking God to surround him with Godly men. So, right now, get on the phone or go knock on a door. Don't quit until you've got four and added them to the "favorites" on your phone.

Ready, break!

Chapter 3

STAND FIRM

Finally, be strong in the Lord and in the strength of his might. Put on the whole armor of God, that you may be able to stand against the schemes of the devil. For we do not wrestle against flesh and blood, but against the rulers, against the authorities, against the cosmic powers over this present darkness, against the spiritual forces of evil in the heavenly places. Therefore take up the whole armor of God, that you may be able to withstand in the evil day, and having done all, to stand firm. Stand therefore, having fastened on the belt of truth, and having put on the breastplate of righteousness, and, as shoes for your feet, having put on the readiness given by the gospel of peace. In all circumstances take up the shield of faith, with which you can extinguish all the flaming darts of the evil one; and take the helmet of salvation, and the sword of the Spirit, which is the word of God, praying at all times in the Spirit, with all prayer and supplication. To that end, keep alert with all perseverance, making supplication for all the saints.

—Ephesians 6:10–18

Last chapter, I talked about how the first way to act like a man is to be watchful. In this chapter we'll talk about standing firm in the faith. And to do that, we've first got to take an honest look at sin. My friend Matt Chandler recently preached a sermon out of Hebrews 12 to a bunch of preachers, because sometimes preachers are the worst at listening to themselves. Hebrews 12:1–2 says this: "Therefore, since we are surrounded by so great a cloud of witnesses, let us also lay aside every weight, and sin which clings so closely, and let us run with endurance the race that is set before us." The writer of Hebrews continues, "Looking to Jesus, the founder and perfecter of our faith, who for the joy that was set before him endured the cross, despising the shame, and is seated at the right hand of the throne of God."

In short, take sin very seriously. If it is entangling you, get it off of you. Why? Because it'll kill you.

When it comes to sin, John Owen said, "Be killing sin or it'll be killing you." I've said this before, but if you fight the devil in the dark, you're going to get your butt kicked.

And a bunch of my buddies who used to be in ministry are not in ministry anymore because they were so afraid to take the thing that they were wrestling with and bring it into the light, because they were embarrassed. And they elevated their ministry over their relationship with Jesus, which means they put themselves on the throne that is meant only for Jesus.

Often, people will share their mess with me and invite me to speak into it. To probe around. So I do. I tell them what scripture says, we pray, and then a week later when I see them again, I ask, "How're you doing?"

"Oh, I'm just so dry."

"Did you do the things we talked about?"

"No."

"Well, do you want freedom from that stuff?"

"Yes, but—"

"Look man, let me say what others are probably afraid to say. You're dumb. I won't waste my time trying to disciple a demon and I can't cast out dumb. I don't know what to tell you."

You've got to quit doing the things you used to do. Delete the app. Do it right now. Your precious will kill you. If it is causing you or tempting you to sin, eradicate it from your life. And if this means you have to ditch your iPhone for a flip phone, then so be it.

Then, do those things that stir your affections for the Lord.

The Puritans—who famously saw us all as sinners—had words for these things: vivification and mortification. "Vivification" means you do the things that stir your affections for the Lord. And "mortification" means you put to death the sin. "Mortify" means "to kill." You crucify your sin. Daily. I think we need to bring these words back.

The writer of Hebrews gives this in two different categories of things to mortify. First, he says to lay aside every weight. I don't love the translation. "Lay aside" makes it sound like laundry. A better translation is *Get off me!* You know what I'm talking about? Those two are very different.

If you are doing something that is shrinking your heart toward the Lord, then you should get rid of that thing. These could be things like too much Netflix, or maybe you're consumed with a hobby at the expense of meaningful relationships, or everything has to be your way, like you're idolizing your appearance or your clean house or the way your body looks. It could be that kind of thing, or it could be way too much time scrolling. Maybe you're obsessed with cable news. Whatever it is.

You know the thing. It could be a morally neutral thing, but in your life, it is not a good thing. Maybe it's that one drink that turns into way too many drinks. You know what I'm talking about? Self-medicating. Most Christians don't take their sin seriously enough. And what you're supposed to do is not pet a sin, not tame a sin, but kill it.

Matt Chandler reminded us in his sermon that sin is like an apex predator. You've seen the show *When Animals Attack*, right? About the third video, you go, *Not a good idea to pet the bear*. Nah, they don't sell honey, they don't put out forest fires. They eat people. That's what they do, they eat meat and you're just a big skeletal meat pole. And eventually that's what it's going to do. I know you raised it and tamed it and called it Fluffy, but I don't care. It's an apex predator. It kills people. That's just what it does. If you put some nachos right here in front of me, I may not eat them now, but if you come back by two hours later, the nachos will be gone because I, too, am an apex predator, okay?

That's what sin is like in your life. A nacho-eating bear. An apex predator. But we don't take it seriously enough.

Years ago, back in the 1900s, I was a broke college kid, and I met this girl at a mixer at my fraternity house. Now, it was dark and I couldn't make a complete assessment, but things seemed okay and she was cute, so I asked her out. In the light of day I found out that she was missing one half of her left index finger. You might keep that in mind as I tell this story.

Being broke, I had to be creative in our dates, so we went to this place called Maymont Park in Richmond, Virginia, where I was a student. Maybe it was a dollar to get in or something. They had a petting zoo and we liked to pet the goats. They also had fainting goats and they were real strict about your behavior when around the goats. Don't scream. Don't make any sudden movements. Don't scare the goats. Just chill. Which to me meant I was supposed to walk in and scream, "Aah!"

Which of course I did. The goats froze, bleated, and keeled over. Like they got tased. Hoofs pointing at the sky, they looked like dead cockroaches. The girl I was with wasn't much of a fan but I thought it was pretty funny. Cheap, too.

To make things better, for a quarter you could get goat food and feed the goats. So after they woke back up and started walking around, we spent fifty cents on food and starting feeding goats. This place was also a frequent field trip destination for elementary school kids, so there were a bunch of us all feeding these goats with all these little kids standing around. I had an idea that I thought would be hilarious.

I screamed, "Oh no, the goat ate off her finger!" The kids screamed, and the goats were all laid out again. Tased. The girl held up her hands in an attempt to show the kids I was not telling the truth, but that only made it worse. Why? What did every single kid focus on? Right. The missing digit. Kids were running everywhere. Like the zombie apocalypse. It was great fun.

We got kicked out of the goat farm, and she broke up with me, but I tell you all that to tell you this: Remember my brother feeding a roadkilled deer to Mufasa and how he just snapped the doe's head off like it was a peanut M&M? Guess what never happens at the big cat Tiger King farm? Nobody ever jumps inside the fence, grabs the doe, tries to feed it to Mufasa, and then fakes like, *Ha-ha, he bit my finger off. See, no finger.* Not one person ever. Why? Because it's an African lion and you don't jack around with a lion, because he could actually eat your whole head off.

You and I treat the enemy like he's a fainting goat when he's not. He's anything but. Right this very second, he's prowling around like a roaring lion seeking to devour every single one of us. And you fight that enemy in the dark and he'll kick your butt. That's why he's kicking your butt right now. That kind of sin is not to be tamed. It's not to be belittled. It's to be taken out back, and you put a hole in its head once and for all. You mortify that sin. Kill the sin or it'll be killing you.

How do you kill it? You start by being honest. You'll never learn to be free until you learn to be honest. But when you walk in the Spirit, something else happens. Paul says, "But the fruit of the Spirit is love, joy, peace, patience, kindness, goodness, faithfulness, gentleness, [and] self-control" (Gal. 5:22–23). These things are not manufactured from the outside in. If you see this as a list of things to try to do, then you're missing the whole point. If I nail an orange to a two-by-four, it does not make it an orange tree. If you want to produce oranges, or fruit, you must first plant the tree. Which means to sink deep roots. So many Christians have said to me, "I'm just trying to be patient." Think about how ironic that is. They're focused on the fruit. Patience. Not the tree that makes the fruit. In this case, that'd be the Word of God and His Spirit.

In John 15, Jesus uses a gardening analogy and when He does, he's talking about walking in the Spirit. He says to those around Him, "Abide in me and I in you" (v. 4). What does he mean by "abide"? *Get real close to me and I'll get real close to you.* They then ask, how do I do that? *Abide in my Word and I will abide in you.*

Instead of trying to manufacture fruit on your own, dig your roots into the Word, into Bible study, into fellowship with other believers, into worship. Get really close to Jesus, and stay there, and He will produce the fruit. If you understand gardening, you know that you can't simply feed the things you want, you've got to take out the things that rob. Weeds, dead branches—you've got to prune and keep out anything that competes with whatever you are trying to produce in your garden. You have to actively maintain your garden, which is you. You have to actively mortify those things that draw your affections away from Jesus.

Let me bring us back around to our verse. I know it feels redundant, but I'm going to keep hammering it so you'll remember it. First Corinthians 16:13–14 says, "Be watchful, stand firm in the faith, act like men, be strong. Let all that you do be done in love."

If the hub and the center of the wheel is "act like men," then the imperatives around it are how we are to act like men. In the current cultural discussion about manhood, there are two extremes, and we need to reject both. The first is this super-chauvinistic macho-man thing that says your manhood is tied up in the price of your car or your popularity on your socials or how much you can consume or the size of your arms. We've also got to reject the opposite extreme that says there are no differences between men and women. That we're just all the same. That's a lie from the pit of hell. Kindergartners can tell the difference; it's we adults who are having trouble. To straighten this out, we look to the Word of God, to the Creator of males and females to figure out what a man is and what biblical manhood is.

Remember how I told you, "The most important thing about you is what you think when you think about God"? I'd like to change that just a little bit and ask you this: When you think about Jesus and who Jesus is, what comes to your mind? Because that might shape you more than anything else. Maybe one of the reasons a whole bunch of men have abdicated their roles at home, peaced-out and chosen to act like immature schoolboys rather than men, is because we don't have a real picture of who Jesus was.

No kidding, most artistic renderings of Jesus that I've seen in churches depict this kind of effeminate little Swedish guy that's never been in the sun and winces at the thought of a hangnail. He's got long, flowing blond locks with no split ends, a Miss America sash, and he's wearing your mom's bathrobe while petting a sheep and singing "Kumbaya" with little kids. Most men I know see that and think, *If that's what it is to be a Christian, I don't think I'm gonna be one of those. I'll pass.* I don't blame you.

For those of you that like those paintings, I hate to break it to you, but Jesus did not have blond hair and fair skin. He was Hebrew. A Jew. Have you seen Middle Eastern Jewish men and women? Blond hair's not really in their gene pool. And as for the effeminate part, the Bible says this in Exodus 15:3: "The Lord is a warrior, the Lord is his name" (NIV).

My seminary experience was not all that great. In fact, it was terrible. It was very liberal and most everybody was a wuss, making apologies for scripture and everything in it. They got tired of me because I told them, "You're a wuss." They almost didn't let me graduate; then they realized I'd have to stay longer and they rethought their position—"Congratulations, Mr. Martin. You are out of here"—so it worked out. I literally had professors saying, "We should remove all of the war language from the Bible." What? I sat there scratching my head. This was back when I had hair. "Um, excuse me, but I don't think God asked your opinion about editing His Word." The Bible talks a lot about war because we were born into a war and we are in one now and will be until either Jesus takes us home or returns. Either way, we're in a war.

Because the Lord is a warrior and the Lord is His name, and you were created in His image, then you are a warrior if you follow in the name of Jesus. Remember, God's plan was for man to have a will to obey, work to enjoy, and a woman to love. And everything went amazing for about a page in the Bible. Then the enemy came along, the serpent of old, took a good gift from God and twisted it, perverted it. As a result, every single one of us is born behind enemy lines, into the kingdom of darkness. That's our starting point.

Men are given strength, not for our own benefit and not just for the sake of fighting. We are given strength to fight on behalf of those who God has put under our authority and under our responsibility. Just look around our current world at what the enemy is trying to take from us. We see the enemy's vision statement in John 10:10—*The enemy comes to steal, kill, and destroy.* If you don't believe that there is an enemy trying to steal your hopes and dreams, trying to destroy your family and kill everything that is good and right and decent, honestly, you're too dumb to talk to. This is why you're getting your butt kicked.

Do you know what a sucker punch is? It's when someone gets punched when they didn't realize a fight was about to happen. If you are not aware that you and I have an actual enemy—the prince of darkness—and that he wants to kill you, then you are the sucker. I mean, let's be honest. The conditions in this world are not just the result of poor decisions. The genocide in Rwanda is not because somebody just made a poor decision. The holocaust against the unborn is not about reproductive rights. The mutilation of boys and girls at the hands of health care providers is not about self-expression. The open mocking of Jesus the Son of God is not about creative expression. It's because there is evil incarnate and it is our enemy.

The question, then, is simple: If we don't stand up and fight against him, who will? In the last chapter, we talked about the schemes of the enemy and how he comes after the defenders because if you can take out the defenders, that leaves those people who are defenseless.

But if you are watching out and paying attention, what does it look like to stand firm in the faith? Some translations translate "stand firm" as "to not give ground, to stand up, to take a stand when the enemy attacks."

Great. But how do we do that?

The reality is that you have been given authority. Maybe you've heard the phrase that the husband is the spiritual leader of the home. That is partially true. He is the leader of the home, and leading spiritually is one part of the job. He is the head. Responsible for it all. And so how do you lead responsibly? What does it look like to stand firm, to fight for the faith of the people that God has put around you?

In Luke 11:21, Jesus says this: "When a strong man, fully armed, guards his own palace, his goods are safe." That means you are the gatekeeper of your home, and a part of what you do is stand at the door of your house and give permission for someone to enter.

Jesus then says, "But when one stronger than he attacks him and overcomes him, he takes away his armor in which he trusted and divides his spoil" (v. 22). That word "divides" means "has his way with his spoils." That doesn't just mean he divides up his stuff; that means the enemy has his way with his wife and his kids. In our culture and in our country right now and all over my city, Jacksonville, the enemy is having his way with a bunch of people who God put under our protection because men have not stood up and fought.

Countless women and children have grown up in pain and loss because the man that God put to defend their home and their hearts did not do his job. Either he got obsessed with some stupid hobby, fell in love with somebody else, or he was just a wuss. The Bible says that the man who will not care for his family is worse than the unbeliever. Just let that sink in. Unbelievers go to hell. This is a really big deal.

The question then is, how do I fight for and defend those I love? I'm glad you asked. We're going to find the answer in Ephesians 6. This is the preeminent text on what it means to fight against this enemy that wants to kill you and steal from you and destroy you.

Pick it up in verse 10: "Finally..."

Now, hold it. If a verse starts "finally," we need to understand why, so let's back up into chapter 5 verse 21: "[Submit] to one another out of reverence for Christ."

From there, Paul spends the next three sections instructing the church at Ephesus how to be married, how husbands and wives should treat each other, how parents and children are supposed to get along, and then how bond servants should serve their masters and masters their servants. With the most important relationships of our lives as the background, we come to chapter 6 verse 10. "Finally, be strong in the Lord and in the strength of his might."

You should know from the beginning, fellas, that this is not about your own strength, and that should give you great relief. In the next chapter we're going to unpack what it means to be strong in the Lord, so stay tuned. But here, it says, "Be strong in the Lord and in the strength of his might." And then here it is, verse 11: "Put on the whole armor of God, that you may be able to stand against the schemes of the devil." This is a very similar command to what we get in 1 Corinthians 16:13 where he says, "Stand firm in the faith." But in Ephesians 6, Paul is going to tease out how you stand firm.

Whenever I teach the Bible, I always want the Bible to be commentary unto itself. Meaning, before I read what other people think about a passage, I like to see what the Bible itself says about the Bible, because ultimately it all has the same author. Right here, Paul is going to give us some how-tos. How do you stand against the schemes of the devil? It doesn't just mean stand up out of your chair. It means take a stand. Don't give ground. Don't back down when the enemy punches you. And part of taking a stand is punching back. To stand means to stand up and fight.

Notice that the devil has schemes or plans. The Greek word for "schemes" is the root word from which we get our word "method." In other words, the enemy's been watching game film on you. He knows where you're weak. He knows your temptations. A great question to ask yourself in your fight against the enemy is this: If I were the devil, how would I fight against me? The answer to that question is probably the area where you need to fight hardest. I know it is for me. So how do you stand against the schemes? The enemy very rarely stands toe-to-toe and launches a full-frontal attack. You can see that coming. It's difficult to miss. If he were to attack us that way, we'd just run into the arms of our heavenly Father, and he'd launch a lightning bolt from on high, kicking tail. The enemy knows he can't defeat the Father in a straight-up fight so he tricks us and draws us into darkness with what's called "temptation."

Here's the reality about temptation. It's tempting. Sometimes the Bible will call it "the lure of temptation." Like a bass fisherman with a lure, you are tempted to follow something into a place you shouldn't go. Think about all that clickbait on Instagram. That's all it is. Temptation from the pit of hell. Conversely, if you're not experiencing temptation, and the enemy is not coming after you, you legitimately have to ask yourself, "Whose team am I on?" If you do not feel an incredible force of a current of culture against you, then it could be because you're just going with it and you're a starting member of his team. Which is not good.

In Ephesians 6:12, Paul says, "For we do not wrestle against flesh and blood—" these are fighting terms "—but against the rulers, against the authorities, against the cosmic powers over this present darkness, against the spiritual forces of evil in the heavenly places." The problems in your life are not the people in your life. They are not your enemy. Your problem is not your boss. Your problem is not your kids. Your problem is not a politician. And it's not your wife. You and I battle not against the flesh-and-blood people in our lives but against spiritual forces.

Now, fellas, let me warn you of something. Later this week when your wife's getting on your nerves and you hear that drip, drip, drip, don't point your finger at her and say, "There you go again, baby.

Pastor Joby said you're possessed by the devil." I'm just telling you, don't do it.

There are two extremes in this argument, and both are dangerous. If you think there's no enemy, no devil at all, he's got you hooked and you're dead already. The opposite extreme is if you think every struggle is a spiritual problem. Sometimes you just run into bad traffic and you should consider leaving the house a little earlier. You're not being attacked by the devil. Sometimes at the end of one of our services, people come to me for prayer—"Pastor, the enemy's attacking me"—and then they proceed to tell me about the attacks, but I think their problem is not the enemy but self-inflicted wounds. Let's don't give the enemy credit for stuff that's our fault.

Because we don't wrestle against flesh and blood, our problem is not the people living under our roof; our problem is a very real enemy who wants to steal, kill, and destroy, and the moment you stop fighting with your wife and fighting with your kids and fighting with your neighbor, you can look around long enough to identify the real enemy and start fighting him. Problem is, you can't see him, so you've got to fight him with unseen weapons.

For those of you scratching your heads, wondering how you do that, these next few verses are a play-by-play game plan into the enemy's playbook. I am not pretending to tell you that this is all this passage means, but I am going to give you some pragmatic tactics as to how you can take the whole armor of God and apply it to what it is like to be a man, husband, and dad today. Here's how you stand against the enemy.

Verse 13: "Therefore take up the whole armor of God, that you may be able to withstand in the evil day, and having done all, to stand firm." In other words, Paul's locking arms with you. *You got this, bro, okay? You've got this.* And when he says "stand firm," it's like a trainer telling a boxer to put his weight forward, on his toes. Lean into it. Because no one ever won a fight from their heels. "Stand therefore, having fastened on the belt of truth" (v. 14).

If you're not familiar with this passage, if you're new to the Bible study, Paul is writing this from a Roman prison. He's probably chained to a Roman soldier, and he's looking at the armor of that soldier and applying physical armor to spiritual battle. Paul was also a master Bible scholar, and he was going back to Isaiah 59, where the author describes the victorious conqueror dressed for battle. He's telling us how we should dress ourselves for battle. And he starts with the belt. The belt of truth.

Which is spot-on in today's world, because if anything is under assault, it's truth. One of the foundational truths in God's creation is that women are women and men are men. That's how He created them. Period. Genesis 1:27 says, "So God created man in his own image, in the image of God he created him; male and female he created them." Male and female were God's idea.

And since that moment, that's been true. Then all of a sudden, we find ourselves in a world where we are told women are no longer women and men are no longer men and not only that, but you get to determine which you are based on how you feel. Foundational truth is under an all-out assault. We are in a truth battle. A battle for what is true. Our world tells us there is no such thing as truth, which is odd because that is a truth claim in and of itself. The person who tells you there are absolutely no absolutes is making an absolute statement—which itself is a contradiction and proves there are absolutes.

As Christians, we fight for truth based not on our preferences but based on the precepts of God. Not because I think they're right or wrong. It does not matter what I think. What matters is what God thinks and what God says. That matters most. Regardless of what the Supreme Court decides. And that's a terrible name for a court because they're not supreme. They don't get to define things that God defines. As Christians, we don't believe that all opinions are equal. Some matter more than others, and God's matters the most. Because of this, we stand up for the truth according to the Word of God. God's Word has authority not simply because what it says is true but because it's also trustworthy. Yes, Jesus is who He says He is, and He always keeps His promise, and if you lay your life down on the promises of Jesus, He will never, ever let you down because you can trust Him. The scriptures aren't just factual statements, but they're so trustworthy we can trust our whole lives with them.

If God is the creator of all life, then He knows how to live it better than we do. Don't believe me? Find any person who tried to do money their way instead of God's way, and you'll find a person who wished they hadn't. Find a person who tried to do marriage their way instead of God's way, and you'll find a person who wished they hadn't. Find a person who tried to do sex their way instead of God's way, and you'll find a person full of regret who wished they'd done it God's way. The author of life knows how to do life. The reality for us men is that we have to fight for truth. The question is this: Does your family know truth? And what are you doing about that? Because almost all news, almost every TV show you watch, almost every magazine you read, and almost everything your kid sees on an iPad screen is lying to them.

You're not a cosmic accident, but that's what they're teaching our kids in school. If we teach people they're just animals, and a generation later they act like animals, then why would we be surprised? The reality of the Word of God is that you and I are fearfully and wonderfully made, designed by God. You are a masterpiece of God, and not the label the world gives you. The Word of God says that you're not the label the world gives you, that only Jesus gets to tell you who you are, and that you were created by God on purpose.

What's more, you were not just a choice of somebody else. There are a lot of accidental parents, but there are no accidental children. According to God, every single life matters. Yours included.

What does it look like to fasten the belt of truth and use it when standing firm in defense of your family? First, for the sake of your children, please read the *Jesus Storybook Bible*. It does a great job of telling the story of the Bible, the narrative of the gospel, in a way they can really understand. The reality is, you'll learn stuff, too. Second, identify the lies your wife is buying into and claim the truth to her. One way we do that is to obey Ephesians 5 and wash her with the Word of God. When we do, we bathe her in the truth, and the truth is not a proposition; the truth is a person, and His name is Jesus.

In John 14:6, Jesus says, "I am the way, the truth, and the life. No one comes to the Father except through me." You want to know how to fasten the belt of truth in your house? Point everybody and everything to Jesus. Remember, Paul is in prison, staring at soldiers, and he realizes that for the Roman soldier, the belt was the centerpiece of everything. Take the belt off, everything falls apart. It's hard to fight with no pants on, okay? It just is. The belt is also the thing that the sword hangs on. Remember that when we get to the sword.

The second piece of armor is this: "Having put on the breastplate of righteousness" (Eph. 6:14). This is my favorite one because it gives us this image of the imputed righteousness of Christ. "For our sake he made him to be sin who knew no sin, so that in him we might become the righteousness of God" (2 Cor. 5:21). This means God transfers our sin nature to Jesus on the cross. And Jesus doesn't just carry our sin, He is made sin. In exchange, God credits us, or imputes us, with Jesus' righteousness. This means when God looks down at us, He no longer sees our sin, He sees His sinless Son, and this breastplate of righteousness is the most clear picture I've ever seen of it.

Have you seen a breastplate from the old-school Roman movies? You ever notice how they never make chubby guy breastplates? No actor getting fitted ever said, "I need more here, a little less here." No. Every single one had perfect pecs and twelve-pack abs no matter what sagged beneath. The breastplate covered up the jiggle. This means when we watch the movie, we see this perfect, CrossFit person. I'm now over fifty, but I used to be ripped. Back in the day, no lie, I was yoked. Now my only fitness goal is *Don't be fat*. Some weeks it slides into *Don't be too fat*. Around the holidays it's *Don't look fat in your clothes*. It's just where I am in my life.

But when we put on the perfect breastplate, then God sees us as perfect. That's the imputed righteousness of Christ. And over time—not overnight—what's under there begins to conform to what's been placed on it. The breastplate guards the heart.

Ninety-nine point nine nine nine percent of the time, when I preach, I preach from the ESV. I like it. It's a really good translation because of how closely it tracks with the original language. In other words, the translators haven't put their spin on what it says. Haven't jacked with the meaning. They've tried to be faithful to the original text, word for word, and let the Bible say what the Bible says without apology. But, when I first entered ministry, I taught from the NIV, so sometimes when I bring up a scripture out of memory, I'll do so from the NIV, and Proverbs 4:23 in the NIV says, "Above all else, guard your heart, for everything you do flows from it." Pay attention to the Bible whenever it says, "Above all else," because the Holy Spirit is telling you, *This is the most important thing, pay attention*.

To put on the breastplate of righteousness means that when you put your faith in Jesus, He placed His approval on you. So your past actions and the labels of this world no longer get to tell you who you are. Only the one who purchased you with His blood gets to tell you who you are. And He calls you Beloved. More than a conqueror. He calls you Son.

Let me ask you: Are you guarding the hearts of the people God has put under your care? Let me ask it this way—do you celebrate who your kids are, or what they have accomplished? Because there's a huge difference between their person and their performance, and most parents focus solely on performance, which is a heart-killer in a child. If all you tell them is "Good job on your report card," "Good job hitting the ball," "Good job on [name your task]," then you are un-gospeling your children. I know that's not a word, but you get the point. And guess what? I do it, too. I want my kids to excel at all the stuff, but at the end of the day, that does very little to shape my son's or daughter's hearts with the truth that they are enough just the way they are. That they are loved perfectly because of who God made them to be.

Can you imagine if every teenage girl in the country had a dad who was telling them they're crazy beautiful just the way God made them? Think of the effect of those words on their hearts. It'd change a generation of women. When we only compliment performance, we are hardwiring into their souls the idea that they are noticed and accepted only when they perform in the way that makes us happy. It's as if we're telling them, *For you to have a right standing before me, you must accomplish X, Y, and Z.* That's not fighting for your family. That's crushing their soul. Every time we do that, the enemy is taking some serious ground.

Now, don't take it too far. I'm all for cheering for our kids. And when we do, we need to be screaming our ever-loving heads off. But, regardless of what happens on the field or the stage or wherever they're performing, they need to know that we still love them like crazy and we're massively proud of them even when they don't hit home runs and don't score touchdowns or win first-place ribbons. If your kids think they can disappoint you, then you don't know the gospel and you certainly haven't communicated it to them.

If the gospel is true, then it is impossible for you to disappoint God. Here's what I mean: If Jesus is the propitiation for our sin, and He is ("propitiation" means "a payment that satisfies the wrath of God"), then God cannot be dissatisfied with you. Now, flip that around toward your children. If you are dissatisfied in your child, you're giving them a picture of what the enemy wants them to believe. This is serious business. And it is a soul-crushing scheme of the enemy. When we as dads fail to affirm our kids so that they know we are not dissatisfied with them and they can crawl up into our laps at any time for hugs and kisses, then we allow the enemy access into our Christian home. Our failure in this area is an open door for the enemy to twist the gospel in our kids' hearts and minds. Dads, we need to get this right. We need to grab our kids, haul them up into our laps—I don't care how old they are—hug them for all we're worth, and tell them we're proud of them. This doesn't mean that you don't push your kids to steward well all the gifts and talents that the Lord has given them. It just means that the verdict comes before that performance.

Same thing's true with your wife. Most women find their identity in their looks, by their performance, and by what they do for others. Why? Because it's the lie society tells them. If they measure up in those areas, then they measure up. Otherwise, too bad. Whether they're the CEO of a Fortune 500 company or a stay-at-home mom, they are primarily judged by those three things.

As her husband, are you pointing her to find her identity in Jesus? Because when you do, you're protecting your wife's heart. It's one way you fight for her. This is where Adam got in trouble. He listened to her voice rather than her heart. If you're going to be married to a woman you need to put in the time, become a student of your wife. I said this earlier. Learn the difference between what she's saying with her mouth and what she's saying with her heart. Both matter, but one matters more. Are you listening to your wife's heart and pointing her to the perfect righteousness that she has in Christ? And when she begins confessing feelings based on lies from the enemy, are you helping her understand, through the gentleness of the Holy Spirit, that's not who she is in Christ? That while she may feel one way or the other, her feelings don't dictate what's true? "I don't care what the front of the magazine looks like, here's what and who Jesus says you are. You are fearfully and wonderfully made. And I'm crazy about you. Now, if we need to start going to the gym so we can live longer so we can love each other longer, great. I'm in. But I love the you right here, right now."

Here's one way you can put on the breastplate of righteousness—check on the hearts of your wife and your kids. Do you ask performance questions when you tuck your kids into bed, or do you ask heart questions? And you don't have to be tucking them in. They can be calling from college. Or the home where they live with their spouse. There's no expiration on this. When my kids were younger, and even still today, I try to ask them questions about their hearts so that they can expose the places where they were hurt, where they're mad, where they were sad, and where they were disappointed. That's just a part of what it means to point them to Jesus so that He can let them know that His perfect righteousness covers all their pain. This is one way that we as husbands and dads fight for the hearts of our families.

The next one, if I'm honest, kind of freaks me out a little bit. Because I don't get this right. A lot. In my life, I have much room for improvement here.

Ephesians 6:15 says, "And, as shoes for your feet, having put on the readiness given by the gospel of peace." Here's what this means: Do you bring peace or chaos to the circumstances you walk into? Shoes take you somewhere and into something. So when you walk into your home, does it become more peaceful or more chaotic? Do things calm down or escalate? If you're going to fight for your family, you should be an ambassador of peace every time you walk through the door. Are you?

The phrase "the gospel of peace" means that by the life, death, resurrection, and return of Jesus, we have been put at peace with God, and because of that we can now be ambassadors of His peace. Think about it, through Jesus, we have been reconciled to God. He has brought us back into relationship with God the Father. Is there an area in your family life for which you need to seek reconciliation? Are you the reason for a broken or wounded relationship? You got a temper? Do you raise your voice when you don't get your way? Are you the reason for the sound of crickets in your house? If you're the man, the husband, the dad, then you need to go first and be the chief repenter in your home. Your kids should learn what repentance looks like from you because you have modeled it for them. If you're waiting on your wife to apologize, then you are failing at your job and you don't get it.

Reconciliation is made up of two ingredients: confession and repentance. Just those two. Which means we men should be the chief apologizers. And if you think, "Well, it's not my fault," then let me lead you back to Ephesians 5. Husbands, lay down your lives for your wives as Christ did for the church. "Yeah, but you don't know my wife." Stop. We don't apologize so that our wife will. And we don't apologize because she should. We confess and repent because Jesus commands it. Period. When Jesus was on the cross, whose fault was that? Jesus chose our imputed righteousness over Him getting to be right. Our sin was not His fault, and yet He took full responsibility for it on the cross. That is how we are instructed to love our wives.

What if Jesus used that line with us? What if He would've loved His bride the way we love our bride? "Yeah, as soon as you get your act together, then I'll do something for you." Guess what? We'd all be dead and going to hell. But He who had no sin made our sin problem His problem, and when He did, He said, "I'm going to take full responsibility for all this."

And here's the thing—none of it, not one single bit, was His fault. He paid the price for stuff He didn't do. And He did it willingly and without opening His mouth to complain. If you're thinking, *Man, this sounds hard*, yep, it is. So was His dying on the cross and paying the penalty for all the sin of all mankind.

Do this. Ask your wife, "When I walk into the house, do I bring peace or chaos?" Ask, "What is it like to be on the other side of me?" And then listen to her response. None of us get it right all the time, some of us don't get it right some of the time, so listen to the words she says, both with her mouth and her heart, and then repent where you need to. Trust me, things will go much better at home if you do.

Ephesians 6:16 tells us, "In all circumstances take up the shield of faith, with which you can extinguish all the flaming darts of the evil one." Notice the "In all circumstances" part. It doesn't say most of the time, or sometimes, or many of the times, it says "all." And just to be clear, "all" means "every single circumstance." The alternative to the shield of faith is not doubt, it's fear. And don't miss the obvious—if you're not walking in faith, then you are walking in fear. I get it. I know you're afraid. Do you know how I know you're afraid? Because I am, too. I don't want to be a disappointment. Don't want to be a letdown to my family, my wife, my church, or you.

One of the great things about pastoring our church is that I get access to some of the best pastors in the country. One of those guys is Matt Chandler, who I mentioned earlier. Matt is a pastor in Texas, a good friend, and one of my favorite pastors on the planet. Because he's been doing this lead pastoring thing longer than I have, I get to bounce questions off him. In most cases, he's been there, done that, and got the T-shirt to prove it. One day I was peppering him with questions when he interrupted me: "What's your biggest fear?"

And because I can trust him and he won't judge me, I answered honestly, "Man, I'm just, I'm just afraid I'll let God down."

To which he kind of shrugged and said, "Bro, you're not holding him up."

I praise God for Matt because in a split second he helped lift the pressure off.

Here's the reality of the world in which we find ourselves—the opposite of faith is not doubt, the opposite of faith is fear. Fear paralyzes and faith moves to action. To take up the shield of faith means that you take action in your family, in your church, in your community. We know the fiery darts are coming—that's a given—so what do we do? Paul, writing this passage in prison, is trying to help us address this.

I know most of you have probably seen or heard of the movie *300*, which depicted rather effectively how the Spartans perfected the shield wall. Because it was so effective as a military tactic, the Romans borrowed the technique. In the first century, Roman soldiers locked their shields together to create one larger unit that moved as a whole. Those soldiers took ground behind the shield because every time they took a step, they closed the distance to the enemy, whose arrows were unable to penetrate their shields.

Paul is sitting in prison, staring at a Roman soldier, thinking, *Our life of faith is just like that. That shield represents our faith. And our faith is the thing that douses the enemy's attack* (Eph. 6:16). And if one shield can defeat the enemy's scheme, then a bunch of them locked together can take back ground that fear had lost.

Do you have a band of brothers who can lock shields with you? Be honest. Friends you can call up and say, "Look, here's my number one fear." And then speak the fear out loud. Sometimes when we're tired and our faith has been taking a beating, we need our brothers to come in and hold their shields over us. This was what the four who brought the paralytic to Jesus did. The Bible says that when Jesus saw their faith, the faith of the four, He healed the paralytic. It was his brothers' faith, and sometimes we just need that. So, in all circumstances, take up the shield of faith.

Verse 17: "And take the helmet of salvation." Part of the reason I think Paul says it's the helmet of salvation is because you can't lose your salvation any more than you can lose your head and still be walking around. If the head goes, you go. You're done. The helmet protects the head, which commands the body, and while you can do without certain parts of the body, you can't do without the head. The helmet of salvation helps us "destroy arguments and every lofty opinion raised against the knowledge of God, and take every thought captive to obey Christ" (2 Cor. 10:5).

In my own life and in the lives of most every man I know, the mind is the battlefield. Where the breastplate of righteousness guards our heart, the helmet of salvation guards our mind, keeping us focused on Jesus, which means that every time we buckle on the helmet of salvation, we counter the attacks of doubt, fear, anxiety, worry, lust, and every other unclean thought.

Let me press you a little further and ask you to think beyond yourself. Does your family know the gospel? Do they strap on the helmet of salvation? Now, to be clear, we can't save anyone. God alone does that. But we can make the introduction, and we can model what it looks like to follow Jesus, we can tell them about the one we love, and they can experience the love He pours through us and into them. I know that when I say this, some of you cringe because you shared the gospel, you followed Jesus, you prayed your face off, you did all the things, and yet your prodigal walked away. Gave you the finger. I get it. There's no pain like kid pain. This just means they're not there yet and we will keep praying. I know a lot of people who were and are good, Godly parents and their kids have, at least for the time being, walked away from Jesus. The enemy wants you to think it's your fault. Your Father wants you to know He's got them. You just keep following Him and we will keep praying.

For those of you soon to be parents or still trying to figure it out, let me encourage you to cast an eternal vision for your family. Many of us reading this are more concerned about our kids' occupations, what they'll do for the rest of their lives, how much money they'll make doing it; will it provide for them all the stuff we want them to have, rather than where they're gonna spend eternity? I realize some things do have to get done, and applying to college is one of them, but are you more concerned with that application or their applying the Word in their own life? One matters a little. The other matters a whole lot. With your calendar and your checkbook, have you communicated and cast an eternal vision? Are the boys in your home preparing to be the men they will become?

Here's the truth—you don't want to fight a brother who has an eternal vision. In Philippians 1, the apostle Paul says "To live is Christ, and to die is gain" (v. 21). How do you fight that guy? You don't wanna fight a guy who enjoys a couple of punches first, right? You don't want to play chicken with a dude that rips off a steering wheel, throws it out the window, and says, "Come on! I been waiting on this a long time."

You'd get out of his way. "All right, you got me. You win."

That's what Paul is saying. He's sitting in prison, staring at what may be the end of his life, and he says, "If you're gonna kill somebody, kill me first. I'm ready to see Christ face-to-face. If not, then get out of my way, I've got kingdom work to do." If you want to be dangerous for the kingdom of God, live with and cast an eternal vision for you and your family.

Ephesians 6:17 continues, "And take the helmet of salvation and the sword of the Spirit, which is the word of God." I cannot communicate this enough. Dads, men, it is your job to teach the Word of God to your entire family, and you cannot teach what you do not know. When Jesus was attacked by the enemy, He replied the same way, *It is written, it is written, it is written*. Meaning, you've got to know the Word and how and when to speak it into your family's life.

One of my best friends, Pastor Ryan Britt, says this: "In regards to eternity, maybe the most important words in the Bible are this, 'It is finished.' In our day-to-day life, maybe the most important words in the Bible are this, 'It is written.' You better have some 'it is writtens' in your life."

Usually, at this point, some guy who's slightly shaking his head raises his hand and says, "But Pastor, I can't memorize stuff." That's just a lie. You remember what's important to you. I'm telling you, man. You're riding down the road, and all of a sudden you hear the first few chords of a song you haven't heard since '86 and yet you can sing every word of it. A part of our job as husbands and fathers is to plant the Word of God—which, by the way, according to Hebrews, is living and active. Think about that. It's alive. And it can do things in your life that you just can't do.

Every year we do a bunch of men's retreats at our church's retreat center. Here's one of the ways I know the Bible is alive. Throughout the weekend, I give no gospel presentation, no salvation invitation. I never have on the men's retreat. All we do is put dudes in a deer stand for four hours with a Bible. I say, "Read this, answer this question," and every year brothers get saved. Explain that to me if this is not a supernatural, inspired document from our Almighty God.

Again, the reason the Word has authority is not just because it contains true statements, but because it is trustworthy. We need to plant the Word of God deeply into the lives of the people that we love. Every night when I tuck my little girl into bed, we pray out loud Psalm 139:14. *Dear God, I praise you because I am fearfully and wonderfully made. Your works are wonderful, I know that full well.* We pray this because my sweet fourteen-year-old one day will be an adult and the world does not want her to believe that. And when some mean girl or soon-to-be-very-sorry little boy tries to tell her anything other than that, I want her to know that what God has said about her is good and true. Not the opinions of others. But my real hope is the Word of God will be so deeply ingrained in her heart that she understands on a soul and heart level that she is fearfully and wonderfully made and that His works are wonderful. So little Scooter can either get on board with that or date somebody else.

This is why I say I don't care about your feelings, because our feelings are not our Lord. We have all kinds of feelings, and while feelings aren't bad in and of themselves and God did give them to us to help us navigate this thing called life, that does not mean they are always true. Feelings lie. A lot. Just ask King David. So instead of being beat around by your feelings like a ship tossed at sea, we stand on the solid rock of the Word of God. He is our anchor.

When my son JP was younger, I'd tuck him into bed and we'd pray Psalm 1 and Joshua 1:9, among other scriptures. Did it for ten years. As he got older, he started playing all-star baseball. Well, if you have any experience with all-star or travel baseball, you know that some of the teams don't really stick within the rules. We traveled to a game where the average age on the opposing team was nineteen and all the kids are jacked up on steroids and pulling up to the game in a Trans Am. When JP got up to bat, the opposing pitcher was six foot three, had a Duck Dynasty beard, and was throwing 600 mph. I was watching JP, and his lips were moving as he stepped into the batter's box. Kid wound up, threw something so fast I couldn't ever see it, and JP sent it to the wall. Free trip around the bases. Have a nice day. When he got back to the dugout, I asked him, "What were you saying?"

"Oh, I was saying my verse, 'Be strong and courageous, do not tremble or be afraid. For the Lord my God is with me.'" Now, just because you memorize a verse doesn't mean you send it into the upper deck, but it does mean you can face what looks like impossible odds with the assurance that God Almighty is standing there with you.

Dads, you have got to plant the Word of God in your kids.

Ephesians 6:18 says, "Praying at all times in the Spirit, with all prayer and supplication." One of the primary ways that you can fight for your wife's heart is say, "Let me pray for you." And I mean, go to war for her in prayer. And I don't mean to pray for you in your prayers for her. You know, "Dear God, please help her calm down." That is not what I'm talking about. Pray for her out loud. Let her hear you say the words. I know some of you are wanting to push back right here: "I ain't good at praying." Stop. Man up. You would never say to your boss, "Well, you know, these reports are not all that great but we both know I'm not good at these reports." You'd get fired. The stakes here are infinitely higher in your home than whatever you're trying to sell at work, so figure it out. Pray the Lord's Prayer over her. Get in a disciple group, and when it comes time to voice prayer requests at the end, say, "I need to know how to pray for my family. Can someone help me?" They will help you.

We will help you. And you will always be willing to get help with something that is important to you. This is more than important.

In every one of my books, I end each chapter with a prayer. Written out. Just turn to the back of any chapter and read those prayers out loud over her. Pretty soon, you'll get the hang of it. One of the primary ways you can fight for your family is to pray for them and over them—out loud.

Midway through verse 18, Paul says, "To that end, keep alert with all perseverance." Perseverance is not all that popular in our current culture, but it has biblical value. To do something for a long time, to work at a job for forty years, our whole society doesn't know what that means right now, but in the Bible, God blesses perseverance. Here's what this means. Just because you're reading these pages doesn't mean you're going back to your family and everything's all of a sudden going to get better. Jesus is not a genie in a bottle. He's a sovereign God, and according to the book of James, He might drag you through the pain cave so He can mature you into the man that He wants you to be.

Don't miss that—God uses your pain for His glory and your good. And when He does, He wants you to persevere. To hang in there. Stick with it. Why? Because He's building something in you more valuable than gold, which is your faith, and it doesn't come cheap or easy. Faith is forged. Not faked.

Then Paul says this: "Making supplication for all the saints, and also for me, that words may be given to me in opening my mouth boldly to proclaim the mystery of the gospel, for which I am an ambassador in chains, that I may declare it boldly, as I ought to speak" (Eph. 6:18–20).

So men, fight, fight, fight with the weapons of war that the Almighty God has given us for the people whom God has placed in your life, that you are the gatekeeper and it is your job to keep out the enemy from your house.

One of the happiest days of my life was the day I found out Gretchen and I were having a boy. We walked out of the hospital and I dialed my dad, "Daddy, I made a boy."

He laughed. "I knew you had it in you, son." All right?

I'm Joseph Perry Martin III, although I was almost Junior Junior, which is just what happens where I'm from. When JP was born, we named him Joseph Perry Martin IV because we're really into us.

But then the most terrifying moment was when we found out we were having a girl. It'll just change you. It does. Everybody needs a little girl. Gretchen looked at me and said, "You okay?"

I said, "I will be."

"What do you mean?"

"We gotta get ready."

Then she was born and Gretchen handed me this little burrito of love and I knew right then that I'd die for this little girl. The first time I held her I told her, "I would die for you. And I might make someone die for you."

As JP grew, I taught him how to keep an eye on his sister. As he got older, I'd ask him, "What's your number one job?"

He'd say, "Protect Reagan."

Straight up, I taught him, "I don't care where you are, if some little punk goofs around with her, puts his hands on her, you make him stop."

Gretchen said, "But they might kick him out of school."

"They might, but guess what I'm gonna do? I'm gonna take him to Disney World. That's how that works."

Men, your number one job is to provide for and protect whomever it is that God has put under your authority. As for the fight, C. S. Lewis said it this way: "My prayer is that when I die, all of hell rejoiced that I am out of the fight." Could you say that about yourself? My prayer is that when I die, hell throws a party because they know they don't have to put up with me anymore. Not because of me, but because of His might and strength.

So here's the point. "The LORD is a man of war; the LORD is his name." That's Exodus 15:3. "So God created man in his own image." That's Genesis 1:27. "For we do not wrestle against flesh and blood, but against the rulers, against the authorities, against the cosmic powers over this present darkness." That's Ephesians 6:12. You put all those together and here's how I sum it up: Bow to Jesus, then stand up and act like a man. Dress yourselves for battle and go to war to defend and protect our loved ones. Stand firm because our victory is in Jesus.

Now here's the thing: Some of you are like, "Ummm, I don't know if I can do it." You're right. You can't. That's the reality. Trying harder will get you nowhere. You have to do this in God's strength and not your own. The eternal reality is that God always confirms who He calls, and because He has called you, you can be certain that He has equipped you, appointed you, and anointed you. And His divine power has given you everything you need to accomplish everything that He has called you to do.

I can already hear the negative responses. "Yeah, Pastor, you don't know my story." Right, and you don't know mine either. But look through the stories of the Bible. Jacob was a cheater, Peter was a coward, David had an affair, Noah got drunk, Jonah ran from God, Paul was a terrorist, Gideon was insecure, Thomas was a doubter, Elijah was moody, Jeremiah was depressed, Moses stuttered, Zacchaeus was short, Abraham was old, Lazarus was dead, and Samson had long hair. The Bible is full of misfits. And what's crazy is that God intentionally uses each and every one for His glory and His kingdom.

And yet, God gave these men what they did not have in and of themselves because He is a good dad and He loves us. And here's what Colossians 2:14 says: "By canceling the record of debt that stood against us with its legal demands." In other words, when the enemy comes against you and says, "This is why you can't do it. This is why you can't stand firm in the faith," you can tell him to shove it. Colossians 2 then says, "This He set aside, nailing it to the cross" (v. 14). Jesus takes all those whispers that the enemy tries to put into your ear and He nails them to the cross. "He disarmed the rulers and authorities and put them to open shame, by triumphing over them in him" (v. 15). You get that? He *disarmed*, past tense. He disarmed the rulers and the authorities, and He put them to open shame.

Men, you do not fight alone. You should have your brothers beside you and the Holy Spirit in you. The Spirit will empower you to bow to the King and then stand up and act like men in the lives of the people that He has put under your care. This means every single day when you lift your head up off that pillow, put on the whole armor of God. Don't get out of bed without it.

One of the ways you can do this is to read Ephesians 6 every single day and remind yourself to armor up. And then set your heart and mind to go to war in truth, in love, and in prayer. When you do this, you will begin to lead and love well, and the people in your homes will flourish. And then something really cool will happen. You will get to see those you love become the men and women God has called, appointed, and anointed them to be.

PRAY WITH ME

Our good and gracious heavenly Father, God, we love You because You loved us first and You went first because You are first. And God, I'll go first and admit that I get scared. Sometimes, I'm afraid to step into what You've called us to do. Oftentimes I'm lazy instead of getting dressed for battle. God, I take my eyes off of the eternal vision that You have for us and I just get worried about my own comforts or my own bruised ego.

And Lord, I confess and I repent when I have shirked the responsibility of being the man that You have called me to be. God, I thank You that it is not up to me and my strength, but I can trust in the perfect God-man who went before me and died on the cross, and the Spirit of your Son lives in me. It's the same Spirit that resurrected Jesus from the grave, that overcame sin and death. You did it two thousand years ago, God, and you still do it every single day in my life.

God, it is my prayer that by the power of Your mighty hand, I will fight so hard that I will endure to the end, and that on the day I die hell will rejoice because I am no longer in the fight. Lord, I pray that our homes, our churches, our cities, and our world will look different because men stood firm and acted like men. We pray this in Jesus' name. Amen.

DOING THE STUFF

Since you now have four brothers you're meeting with weekly, the five of you need to pray Ephesians 6 out loud. You need to learn to armor up. And it's okay if you don't get it right the first time. If it feels awkward and bulky. That's why it's called "practice." But do it long enough and you'll feel naked without it.

If you don't have four friends, then you skipped a step and you need to back up, find four brothers, and ask yourself why you're reading this book. This is not self-help, and it's not seven steps to a better you. This is a battle plan to keep Mufasa from ripping your head off your shoulders. This is a battle plan for how to love and lead well. This is a battle plan to become the man of God that God intends you to become, but passive indifference won't get you there.

I said it in my son's weight room when all the boys were standing around, "Everybody wants to be strong, nobody wants to be sore." Don't be a wuss. Pick up the phone. Knock on the door. Get together. Meet weekly. Zoom if you travel a lot. Admit the stuff that's shameful. Confess the sin. Repent. Then armor up and lay down your life for your wife and children and those you love.

Ready, break!

Chapter 4

BE STRONG

And as Jesus was going up to Jerusalem, he took the twelve disciples aside, and on the way he said to them, "See, we are going up to Jerusalem. And the Son of Man will be delivered over to the chief priests and scribes, and they will condemn him to death and deliver him over to the Gentiles to be mocked and flogged and crucified, and he will be raised on the third day." Then the mother of the sons of Zebedee came up to him with her sons, and kneeling before him she asked him for something. And he said to her, "What do you want?" She said to him, "Say that these two sons of mine are to sit, one at your right hand and one at your left, in your kingdom." Jesus answered, "You do not know what you are asking. Are you able to drink the cup that I am to drink?" They said to him, "We are able." He said to them, "You will drink my cup, but to sit at my right hand and at my left is not mine to grant, but it is for those for whom it has been prepared by my Father." And when the ten heard it, they were indignant at the two brothers. But Jesus called them to him and said, "You know that the rulers of the Gentiles lord it over them, and their great ones exercise authority over them. It shall not be so among you. But whoever would be great among you must be your servant, and whoever would be first among you must be your slave, even as the Son of Man came not to be served but to serve, and to give his life as a ransom for many."

—*Matthew 20:17–28*

Okay, so let's say you've armored up. Now what? Well, for starters, men who put on armor expect to be in a fight. Otherwise, why wear it? And men who expect to fight tend to be strong on some level, because they understand the nature of warfare. Otherwise, men who walk into battle unprepared tend to get their lunch handed to them.

If you're new to this whole walking-with-Jesus thing, or if you've been walking with Him a long time and you just need reminding, here's the simple but often overlooked truth of our lives—we're in a battle against an enemy who's been fighting idiots like us for thousands of years. He's really good at warfare.

Which begs the question: Are you? Not only does our enemy prowl around like a roaring lion trying to take us out and off of our watchful position, he wants those we're called to defend. Last chapter I asked: Okay, if we are going to fight against the enemy, what does it look like to stand firm in the faith? Then we unpacked Ephesians 6, which showed us how to put on the full armor of God so that we can stand against the attacks of the evil one. The next thing Jesus commands us is be strong. And right about here we bump into a problem.

Notice He doesn't say be passive, or be a doormat, or be a wuss. He also doesn't say to be strong in yourself and in the strength of your own might. Jesus says, "Be strong." Our problem is that we have a corrupted idea of strength. In Luke 11:21, Jesus says, "When a strong man, fully armed, guards his own palace, his goods are safe." So, what does it mean to be a strong man? When we think "strength" we call to mind some Hollywood action hero or an MMA cage fighter or CrossFit's Fittest Man on Earth, which means most of us have no idea what it means to be strong in a biblical way.

The dictionary says, "Strength is having the power to perform physically demanding tasks, able to withstand great force or pressure." I think the second half of that definition is probably the most helpful. If you're a Godly man, your enemy the devil is going to place an incredible amount of power and pressure against you. Because if you take seriously the authority given you as a son of the Most High, you're a threat to his kingdom. He's hated you from the moment you were born again. Why? Because if you've surrendered to the Lordship of Jesus, then Jesus has put His very Spirit in you and commanded you to make disciples. Which means you are now playing for Team Jesus and actively working to free slaves from the kingdom of darkness. As a result, he's been actively waging war against you, and most of you are oblivious and have yet to wrap your head around the fact that you have a spiritual, unseen enemy who's as real as you and me and wants you dead. And not only does he want you dead, he wants you to suffer greatly in the process.

So what's the remedy? What's the battle plan? Our world and our culture answers this question with *bigger muscles, more guns, and more worldly power*, all of which are powerless against this enemy. Now, don't get me wrong, I'm all for muscles and I do own a few guns, but those things don't make me a man. They're things I get to do as a man. Big difference.

If we really want to understand what it means to be strong, maybe we should ask the only strong man to ever live who rendered a complete and irrevocable defeat to the enemy. If you go to Matthew 20, Jesus turns the world's entire power paradigm on its head. Let's pick it up in verses 17–19: "And as Jesus was going up to Jerusalem, he took the twelve disciples aside, and on the way he said to them, 'See, we are going up to Jerusalem. And the Son of Man will be delivered over to the chief priests and the scribes, and they will condemn him to death and deliver him over to the Gentiles to be mocked and flogged and crucified, and he will be raised on the third day.'"

This is the gospel of Jesus Christ. Before Jesus redefines what it means to be great, what it means to be powerful, what it means to have strength, he's going to start with the gospel. In other words, what looked like the greatest moment of weakness in the world—that the God-man is going to be falsely tried, convicted of crimes He didn't commit, flogged, and crucified—turns out to be the demonstration of ultimate power and strength. Not just in His day, but throughout all eternity. Jesus wants them to know that He did not show up to flex. He showed up to die. To forgive the unforgivable. To love the unlovable. To demonstrate faith.

And here's what's crazy: The Pharisees, the religious leaders, turn out to be bad guys of the New Testament. They're like the Klingons of the Bible. Part of the evil Empire. Always up to no good. But they weren't stupid. In fact, they were crazy smart. They knew the Bible better than everybody else in town. In fact, the name "Pharisee" in Hebrew simply means "separated ones." Their job was to memorize the Old Testament and keep all the rules; they wanted always to be ceremonially clean so that when the Messiah showed up, they would be the first to recognize him. That was their job. But they made one big mistake. They believed the Messiah was going to show up in power, slinging lightning bolts from on high, not as a servant who would allow Himself to be beaten, battered, bruised, and hung on a cross. Despite all their learning, when Jesus showed up they missed Him. They stood two feet away from him, they could smell the breath of God, and yet they did not know that the Almighty was in their presence.

A part of the reason they totally missed it is because they thought God would demonstrate Himself in power the way He had with the Egyptians. The Pharisees thought the Messiah would kick out the Romans, and the nation of Israel would once again become the mighty nation it had been at one time. But instead of flexing, Jesus, the Passover Lamb who takes away the sins of the world, humbled Himself and went willingly to the cross, and they had no box for this. To them, the cross looked weak.

Verses 20–21: "Then the mother of the sons of Zebedee came up to him with her sons, and kneeling before him she asked him for something. And he said to her, 'What do you want?' She said to him, 'Say that these two sons of mine are to sit, one at your right hand and one at your left, in your kingdom.'" Now, watch what Jesus does here. He's about to redefine what it means to be strong. These two men and their mom want power, position, and strength. And what Jesus does is reorient us into His Father's kingdom. God's economy.

The first thing is this, a strong man is a sabbathed man. Now, I made that word up, but let me tell you what it means.

Even though the mother and her sons had the right motive, their perspective was wrong. Here's what I mean. They knew it wasn't what they could do out there on their own but their proximity to Jesus that determined their success. They knew things would go really great if they could just sit at the right hand and left hand of Jesus. That's why I say a strong man is a sabbathed man. Who even does that these days, right? I mean, most of us don't sabbath. Even though it's a commandment, most of us don't. I mean, the only people I know that sabbath are Hobby Lobby and Chick-fil-A. And we tend to get very frustrated with Chick-fil-A when we want a chicken sandwich and they're closed. Am I right? How many times have you turned into an empty Chick-fil-A parking lot on Sunday? And we think, *Ugh! Sabbath.*

But here's what the sabbath is. The sabbath was and is a gift from God. In the beginning, before there was ever sin, there was a sabbath. God created everything in six days. And on the sixth day, He created the crown jewel of all His creation. He created man and woman in His image and likeness. He formed the man, and He breathed the ruach of life into the man, who then opened his eyes, and the man was face-to-face with His Almighty Father. And then God said, "It's not good for man to be alone," because everybody knows he'd just burn the whole place down, so he gave him a wife to keep him in order. And then the two together were cocreators with God.

And then the next day, what happened? The next day is the sabbath, which means on the first full day of humankind, they experienced sabbath. Why? To rest? No. What from? They weren't tired. They hadn't done anything. You don't get real tired being created, right? They rested on the very first day, which meant that the sabbath is not for us to rest from work, it's for us to rest *for* the work that God has established for us to do for the next six days. You see, it's the first day of Adam and Eve's week, where we give God our first and our best. In the Old Testament, sabbath day was sundown Friday until sundown on Saturday. That all changed for the early followers of Jesus when they moved the primary day of corporate worship to Sunday, the first day of the week, because that was the LORD'S DAY. The day of Christ's resurrection.

The Book of Hebrews says that we find our sabbath rest not in a particular day but in the Risen Christ. Where we reorient ourselves to God through corporate worship and Bible study. Where we gather together as a family. It is about rest where we get poured into, rather than always pouring out. And it's about reorienting ourselves with Jesus. Rooting our relationship with Him. Sabbath is a gift from God. And it is a reminder that you need Him. Every single time you get tired and you need to rest, it is a reminder that you cannot do this on your own.

Throughout all the Old Testament and on into the first century, people were born into an agricultural society, which meant that to take a full day off was a demonstration of faith. When you cut your labor force by one-seventh, what you're saying is this: "God, we can do more with you in six days than we can do on our own in seven days." To sabbath is a declaration that God's still got the whole world in His hands.

When I graduated seminary, my favorite professor told me, "If the enemy can't make you bad, he'll make you busy." So let me just ask you: Are you busy? Most of us value busy. Think about it. When we greet one another, we ask, "You staying busy?" And how do most of us answer? "Uh-huh. Up to my eyelids. Don't know how I'm going to make it." Can you imagine if we answered, "No, actually, I'm not. I live in a perfect six-day rhythm where I enjoy sabbath rest on the seventh." If we actually said that to one another, we'd ask, "What is wrong with you? Are you in a cult? Get away from me."

If the devil can't make you bad, he'll make you busy. So my question is this: Are you spending your most precious commodity, your time, on the most important things? Or are you spending all of your time on the things that don't really matter? Because that says you're trying to prove who you are through your effort and activity instead of trusting your identity in Christ. That your performance determines your worth and not the fact that you're a blood-bought, blood-washed, blood-redeemed son of God. None of us are Superman. We all need to rest. All need to be refueled. All of us are born with the fundamental need to be rooted and restored in and through our relationship with Jesus.

Remember the parable of the talents in Matthew 25? It's one of my favorites. The master gave out three sums of money. Five talents, two talents, and one talent to these three guys. Each according to their ability. And a talent was a very large sum of money. Most likely given in silver coins. One talent equaled six thousand denarii, and one denarius represented a day's wage for labor. So one talent was a lot. Twenty years of wages. The guys with the five and two talents went out and put that money to work. In doing so, they were trusting God with the abilities He had given them and they doubled their money. In contrast, the guy with the one talent was fearful of his master, so he dug a hole and he hid the money. And when his master returns, the five- and two-talent guys brought five and two talents more, to which the master said, "Well done, good and faithful servant. You have been faithful over a little; I will set you over much. Enter into the joy of your master." Then the one-talent guy walked up with his one talent all covered in dirt from where he'd buried it. The master looked at him and said, "You wicked and slothful servant."

Many of us read that and think, *Wow, he wasn't slothful.* Yeah, he was. He was busy burying and hiding and digging. But he was lazy with trusting. He was lazy in faith. But busy in activity. And in truth, he was too busy about all the wrong things instead of trusting God with what he had been given. You see the difference?

So my question is this: Are you busy? Because busy is not good. Well-meaning Christian people tell me all the time, "Pastor Joby, I think you're too busy. You need to slow down."

Jesus hasn't called us to slow down. He doesn't say pace yourself nor does He ask you if you're running at a comfortable pace. A comfortable pace can lead to mediocrity, which sounds terrible. For all you driven men out there, being driven is not a bad thing provided we obey the commandment to sabbath. Otherwise we will burn out, at which point we're no good to the advancement of the kingdom. The Bible says we work and sweat for six days. And then we stop and sabbath. We rest, recuperate, rejuvenate, and stay rooted in the gospel of Jesus Christ so that we can get after it again. The world would have us seek a balanced life, but balance is a myth. Our job is to love God with all our heart, soul, mind, and strength, and work every day as though we're working for the Lord. Then on the seventh day, we stop and sabbath. We rest in Him. Most of us are really good at the working-hard-for-six-days part. And we're really bad at the resting-on-the-seventh-day part.

Sabbath is the fourth commandment, and it's really important. The first three commandments are about our vertical relationship with the Lord. Commandments five through ten are about our horizontal relationships with one another. Thessalonians tells us that the fourth commandment is the hinge commandment, because if you don't reorient yourself to the Lord every seven days, then you will not be able to love people. In other words, like Jesus said, you've got to love God, and love your neighbor as yourself.

Let me ask you again: Are YOU busy? Most of you know the answer without being told. Do you need to stop and rest? Is your activity actually just fueled by your fear that you're going to let somebody down, understanding that it's not you that's holding them up to begin with? I've got a theory. I can't prove it but my theory is this: You know those pastors who are failing morally and disqualifying themselves from ministry? I really believe that their failure has more to do with exhaustion than morality. I think they're just spent. Instead of reorienting themselves on a weekly basis with God and who He is, and orienting themselves as a son, they're really acting like servants trying to prove themselves to the Lord. Which is exhausting. And we men make some of the worst decisions in the world when we're exhausted. When we get tired, just worn out, we snap and react, instead of responding in love.

For all you type A overachievers, I'm not trying to hold you back. I've been accused of being one myself. But if you skip sabbath you are, in fact, saying, *I got this*. Which are the three most dangerous words you can ever say. Truth is, you don't. Never have. Never will.

Only when we surrender and reorient ourselves to Jesus do we remember that He alone has got this and without Him, we're toast. A strong man is a sabbathed man, so stop, kneel before the Lord, rest, and reorient yourself to the gospel of Jesus Christ. Ultimately, sabbath is not an excuse to be lazy; it's a submission to His Lordship.

Secondly, a strong man is a persevering man. Watch how Jesus answers the mother and her two sons in Matthew 20:22–23: "You do not know what you are asking. Are you able to drink the cup that I am to drink?" They say to Him, "We are able." And He said to them, "You will drink my cup."

Notice there are two cups here. There's "the cup that I am to drink" and "my cup." The first is God's cup of wrath, which Jesus alone will drink. As the only sinless man to ever live, He'll drain every drop. The Father's cup of wrath being poured out on sin. It's the same cup Jesus speaks about when He's praying in the Garden of Gethsemane, *Father, if there be any other way, let this cup pass from me; not my will but Your will be done* (Luke 22:42). Which, incidentally, is the same question a lot of people ask these days. The question is this: Why does Jesus have to be the only way to heaven? Can't there be a bunch of ways? Jesus is asking, *"Hey God, if that's true, if Oprah is right, can we go with her plan so I don't have to die on the cross? Seems like an awful waste of my blood if there's another path to You. Not my will, but Your will be done."*

The Father's answer was and is the cross. The only way to satisfy the wrath of God against our sin was for Jesus, who knew no sin, to become sin, and make payment on our behalf. To become the propitiation for our sin. Just to be clear, the death of Jesus is the only acceptable payment that satisfied the wrath of God on our behalf. Jesus was and is the payment that satisfies. That's what "propitiation" means. As a result, we are imputed—which means we are given something we don't deserve—with His righteousness and His perfect life is credited to our account. And because we get credit for His sinless life, when the Father looks at us, He sees His Son's righteousness. This is what's so inconceivable about the cross. That Jesus, because He loves us, did for us what we could never do for ourselves in ten thousand lifetimes.

We get to drink from the cup of the new covenant of grace because at the cross Jesus drank the full cup of wrath for our sin.

The second cup is the cup of the new covenant in His blood. We get to drink from this cup of the new covenant of grace because at the cross Jesus drank the full cup of wrath for our sin. In this cup of grace, He extends forgiveness to us, and then when He's resurrected, He commands us to do the same.

But let's don't sugarcoat it, forgiveness is not easy. In fact, forgiving people who don't deserve it is really hard. When they say, *"Hey, can we sit at your right and left?"* what they're really saying is that they want those positions of power. They want the power that comes with His throne. But what they fail to realize is that when we follow Jesus, we follow Him to a bloody cross. Why? Because there is no glorification without a crucifixion. This is why there were two thieves flanking Jesus. One on His left and one on His right. They are us. We are them. That's where we belong. He knows that every single one of the disciples will be martyred. Following Him will not be easy. It will test them to the end. And in most every case, that end was brutal. Jesus knows that to be a strong man is to be a persevering man. If you are going to stand up and act like a man, you will endure pain. Hardship. Extreme discomfort. And yet, when we follow Jesus, we follow him to and through the cross. Your salvation is free, but living it out may very well cost you everything, and it might hurt in the process.

Being a man is not a pain-free walk down easy street. You will endure pain. What's more, and this may come as a shock to many of you, a man like Jesus takes responsibility for things that are not His fault. That's right, he mans up and owns things he didn't do. That's a big part of what it means to be a man. To bear one another's burdens. It means to take responsibility for things that are not your fault. Men have heard me say this and asked me, "Pastor, what on earth are you talking about?" I point them to Ephesians 5. Paul says, "Husbands, love your wives, as Christ loved the church and gave himself up for her" (v. 25). Stop right there. How did Christ give Himself up for her? Let that sink in, husbands. This means everything in your world is your responsibility, regardless of whether it's your fault or not. Let me make it really practical. Husbands, when you're fighting with your wife, you have two options. You can be right, or you can be married. Those are your options.

Think about it this way: Jesus didn't have to die. He chose to. He could've shown up, taken one look at us, and said, "Nope. Peace out. You guys figure it out. I'm not dying for a bunch of whining losers like you. This is not my fault. It's yours." Jesus could have shown up and demanded to be right, but He didn't. He showed up as Savior. Big difference.

How many times did Jesus sin? None. How much responsibility did he take for sin? All of it. Jesus didn't deserve God's wrath—we do—and yet He chose to endure it on our behalf. The thing that makes you a man is not that you experience pain, but that you can endure and persevere through pain in accordance to what God has called you to do. Being a man doesn't mean you get all the authority and you get to tell others what to do. Being a man means you leverage that authority to endure pain on behalf of others. Proverbs 24:16 says, *The righteous man falls down seven times and rises again*. Perseverance is not a value in our current culture. Very few people keep doing the same thing over and over in our culture. People actually think it's cool today to see how many companies they can work for in a small amount of time. The idea of loyalty never crosses their mind. In my dad's age, it was an honor to spend forty years with one company.

Perseverance is a biblical value. With it, we continue to act like Jesus over a long period of time. Doing so will cost you and it will be painful, and you will be faced with a choice: Endure or not. Will you willfully and willingly choose to endure pain on behalf of others? A few years ago, as a hurricane was approaching Jacksonville, a man in our church went to the beach with his family to look at the waves. It's a Florida thing—unless you live here you won't understand, but we do this. For some crazy reason, we have to see how big and angry the ocean can get just before a storm. Some of the most crazy among us have to paddle out and ride those waves, but that's another book. Anyway, he looked out into the water, and there were two guys on surfboards who weren't going to make it. They were getting crushed by the waves and drowning. So what did he do? Tore off into the water to save them. Problem is that he figured out very quickly that a coming hurricane is no joke and the ocean ain't playing, so now there were three drowning people. But despite the fact that it was really hard, he was helping these two guys make it in. Pretty soon, another surfer threw him a surfboard, and they all made it to shore safely. Everybody cried. It was a moment.

When his friends found out about it, they sent him an email, and most of it read, "Hey man, don't be a hero. Don't try to be a hero. Quit trying to be a hero." To which he replied, "If I'm going to stand up and act like a man, I'm supposed to be the hero, or what the Bible just calls a man." I could not agree more. Although, maybe next time take the board with you. Let's use some wisdom when swimming out into a hurricane.

The point is this: If you're gonna be a man, that means you run toward the pain, not away from it. A. W. Tozer says, "It is doubtful whether God can bless a man greatly until he has hurt him deeply." Chuck Swindoll puts it this way: "When God wants to do an impossible task, he takes an impossible man, and he crushes him. Leave room for the crushing." And persevering will crush you.

To be strong is not necessarily to be tough. It's to be tender for and with the people that God has placed in your life. It is to make yourself vulnerable. It is to expose yourself to great pain and great discomfort for the benefit of the ones whom God has placed in your life. That's what it means to be a man. And when you get knocked down, and you will, then you get up over, and over, and over, and you never throw in the towel. Not ever. Because Christ never threw in the towel for you. He endured the pain and suffering all the way to the cross, and the Spirit of the Son lives in you to persevere.

A strong man is a sabbathed man. A strong man is a persevering man. And a strong man is a humble man. Jesus says, "You will drink my cup, but to sit at my right hand and at my left is not mine to grant, but it is for those for whom it has been prepared by my Father" (Matt. 20:23). Do you see the humility here? At our church, we have a very high Christology. Meaning, we hold Jesus in very high regard. We believe Paul in Colossians when he said that Jesus is before all things. He's preeminent. From the beginning, He created all things by Him, through Him, for Him, and to Him, that God was pleased to have the fullness of Himself dwell in Jesus.

In other words, cosmically and eternally, Jesus is a really, really big deal.

All authority in our heaven and on earth has been placed under Jesus. And then this mom comes forward and says, *"Hey, can you make my sons like senior VPs of Jesus Incorporated?"*

Jesus says, *"That's a little above my pay grade."*

She responds with *"What? I thought you were preeminent."*

He is, and because He is, He does not use His position of authority for Himself. He lays that down in humble submission to His Father.

Let me ask you, do you know how to submit to authority? Or are you grabbing for power? Can you submit to the authority of our government? You should strive to be a good citizen until doing so means you are not being a good Christian. Can you submit to the authority at your work? Can you submit to the authority of the church? Or do you always have to be the boss? What matters more to you, the title or getting the job done?

When Jesus was on trial for His life and Pontius Pilate asked, "Are You the King of the Jews?" He answered him and said, "It is as you say" (Luke 23:3 NKJV). Pilate couldn't understand why Jesus wasn't fighting back. Jesus then said, "You would have no authority over me at all unless it had been given you from above" (John 19:11). Jesus turned the idea of real power on its head. Strength and security are not demonstrated in a show of power. Strength and security are best demonstrated in humility.

My friend Pastor Ryan Britt, a brilliant twenty-first-century theologian, said this one time at a staff meeting: "No one can keep you from what God has for you, and no one can give you what God has not."

Do not expect God to trust you with authority until you learn how to live under authority. You want to stand firm and be a man?

Then you humble yourself to the authority that God has placed over you. I learned this firsthand on the slow play. One of God's great gifts to me is that for a decade I had the opportunity to serve under the authority of Pastor Jerry Sweat at Beach Church in Jacksonville Beach, Florida. The most humble man I've ever met. Literally the best Christian I've ever met in my whole life. I came in as a youth pastor, which is a sweet gig. All the fun of ministry without all the responsibility of being a lead pastor. I thought I was going to be a youth guy forever and work with students forever. My thinking was pretty simple. I thought, *Little kids, they don't know what's going on. Old people, they're too set in their ways. They're done. Eighty-five percent of people surrender to Jesus before they turn eighteen years old. Why waste my time with everybody else?*

Now, here's the other thing. I don't know if you know this about me, but humility is not one of my greatest attributes. I usually have an idea about everything, I think my ideas are best, and I can usually back them up with a Bible verse. That's not always a good combination. I would sit in these church committee meetings thinking my ideas were all the best, and then I'd show up to weekend services with a critical mind and often a critical heart. And here's what I would think: *If I was in charge, this is how I would do it.* And the Lord, seeing my lack of humility, said, "All right, Scooter, your turn."

What I did not realize was that God was placing me, an arrogant, egomaniacal jerk at times, under the authority of one of the kindest, most humble men I've ever known in my life to smooth off some of the rough edges. To be a safe place for me to learn by example what it looks like to humble yourself. To not use your position over people, but to be humble. When we were first starting our church, another local pastor took me to lunch. He had been in ministry a long time, and he said, "Look here, Joby, you honor Pastor

Jerry Sweat, and you honor Beach Church in this season, and God will honor you in your season. And the way you leave this season of ministry determines how you step into the next season of ministry."

I felt like I was having lunch with Ezekiel. I walked out of there, grabbed our team, and took our marching orders straight out of Philippians 2. We should do nothing out of selfish ambition or vain conceit, but consider others in humility better than ourselves. That our attitude should be the same as that of Christ Jesus, who being in very nature God did not consider equality, but He humbled Himself, poured Himself out in obedience as a servant even unto the cross. If you think, *I'm the man*, truth is you're full of yourself. Jesus says, *"You wanna be the man? Pour yourself out in humility."* If you really want to be the man, then humble yourself. One way to know is to ask yourself: Are you constantly self-promoting, or do you actually trust God with your life? Do you constantly attempt to control the outcome? If you do, chances are really good you're not humble.

A strong man is a sabbathed man, a persevering man, a humble man. And a strong man is a serving man. Matthew 20:24 says, "And when the ten heard it, they were indignant at the two brothers." You think? Being indignant is like saying, *What is wrong with you?* You know they had to be thinking, *You gonna send your momma to go talk to Jesus on your behalf?* Verses 25–26: "But Jesus called them to him and said, 'You know that the rulers of the Gentiles lord it over them, and their great ones exercise authority over them. It shall not be so among you.'"

When He says "Gentiles" here, He doesn't just mean those of us who are not of Jewish heritage. He means all people who don't believe in God. People who think they're the God of their own life, who lord it over one another whenever they can. To which Jesus says, "It shall not be so among you." In other words, when we act like that, when we lord our authority or position over another, we are living as a practical atheist—someone who says they believe in God but doesn't look like it or act like it.

When Jesus says, "It shall not be so among you," it causes me to scratch my head. Why? Because it kind of is so with me. I can be as much a hypocrite as anyone. But here's the good news—a hypocrite who admits their hypocrisy is no longer a hypocrite, he's just a sinner. Ding, ding, ding. Winner, winner, chicken dinner. That's me.

If you're uncertain and need help to find where you fall in this continuum, here's a pretty good litmus test for the condition of your heart and whether you're there to humble yourself and serve others or keep it all about you. What do you do when you realize that you are the most influential person at the table? What do you do when you look around and realize you're the big dog, you're the head cheese, you're it? You could be driving the swagger wagon in carpool, coaching your kids' Little League team, or leading a discipleship group, or you may be the CEO at the executive table. Wherever it happens to be, the question is, what do you do when you realize, *Man, I'm the boss?*

Now, confession time. By nature and nurture, you know what I do? I flex. If and when I feel super respected, then it's very easy for me to be gentle and lowly. But when I feel challenged or disrespected, I'm not so Christlike. My knee-jerk is to think, *Dang right I'm the boss. And if you want to continue to live here rent free, you'll do what I say. Why? Because it's my house, and as long as I'm paying all the bills, you live under my rules.*

When Gretchen and I married, I promised myself I would not turn into my dad. Don't get me wrong. He is a good man and a great dad. But as a teenager I made promises to myself that when I walked into the room everyone would relax, not tighten up. "I ain't gonna be like that." Now all I do is walk around the house turning off lights, talking to myself. "Anybody in this room? I guess we're going to air-condition all of Jacksonville." I do, I sound just like him. Perry Martin is just coming through me. I'm confessing it and truth is, I need to go home and, by the power of the Holy Spirit, work on this one. Because currently, I walk into my house and just have expectations that stuff is going to be done for me. I know it's horrible, but I do. I don't want to, I'm working on it, and Jesus is working on me, but it's the truth. Good thing is I'm not alone in this. Do you do that? Do you flex?

In the last decade or so, "servant leader" has become the buzzword. Especially in my world, preacher world. Everybody wants to be seen and known as a servant leader until they're treated like a servant. Then it's not so much fun. The problem we have is Jesus, who did not come to be served but to serve, and offered His life as a ransom for many. These words of Jesus always cut me down the middle: "But whoever would be great among you must be your servant, and whoever would be first among you must be your slave" (vv. 26–27).

Do you see yourself as a leader who sometimes serves, or a servant who sometimes leads? Typically, I see myself as a leader who picks and chooses when I serve. Or when it suits my schedule. Or whatever. You get the point. I mean, I serve my tail off on a mission trip. But do I walk into work, where I am the boss, and expect everyone to serve me? I'm guilty. I'm confessing. Jesus says, *A strong man is a serving man.* This means that if we are "in Christ," our goal is not to rise to the top of the heap, it's to kneel down and to lift others up. Listen, I'm not saying that I don't want you to be promoted. I do. I hope and pray that over time, you're promoted to boss, CEO, CFO, and all the Os. Hope you get all of them. But when you get there, I pray that it is God who elevated you because He finds you worthy of the position, and not you who have elevated yourself.

When we actually trust God and believe that He placed us on purpose, like a city on a hill or like a light that shall not be covered up, then we understand He did this so we can leverage our position for those whom God has put under our authority. Our promotion is not so much about us as about everyone else. Remember that. That's what it means to be a man, according to Jesus. On the night Jesus was to be arrested and tried, He institutes the Lord's supper. It's kind of a big deal. And in John 13, the Bible says, *Jesus, knowing that all authority, all things had been put under his control, got up from the table and showed his disciples the full extent of his love* (John 13:3).

How did He show them? Let's ask the question another way: What did He *not* do? He did not demand that they worship Him. In fact, He didn't demand anything. He did not preach a sermon, as important as sermons are. He did not perform a miracle. He did not map out their future so that they would know exactly what God's will was for their life. He did not explain to them the succession plan after He went away. In that moment, He dressed Himself as a servant, a slave. He tied a towel around His waist, and then the almighty maker of heaven and earth, the one who is preeminent and before all things, knelt down and washed His disciples' feet. We read that and we're sort of numb to it by now. We all know Jesus washed their feet. It just does not hit us with the same impact that it hit the people in the first century. Because in the first century, this was unheard of. Masters didn't do this. It was beneath them.

And think about it—in the first century, feet were nasty. They wore sandals. They walked on dirt roads. And it was an agrarian society, so animals pooped everywhere and all the time. People in the first century did not walk behind their donkeys with a Hefty bag and a pooper-scooper. This is a relatively new phenomenon in our neighborhoods. So where does all that stuff go? Your feet. So peoples' feet were nasty. Or like my people would say, "shnasty." If you add a *sh* on the front of it, it's just worse. Take my word for it.

You starting to get the picture? There were also several ceremonial cleansing rules governing how you came into a home to eat dinner. The rules dictated you wash your hands, but not your feet. Why? They didn't want feet filth transferring to the hands because it would then end up in the food. Everybody ate with their hands, and what's more, everybody double-dipped. It was just how they ate. So, in that environment, Jesus got up to do for them what nobody else wanted to do for them.

Da Vinci's take on the Last Supper was all wrong. In the first century, they didn't sit at a table, all on one side, like they were judging an event. They reclined on the floor. This meant the servant would go behind them and wash the filth off their feet to keep it away from the table. Jesus, their master, leverages His strength not for Himself, but for the benefit of everybody else. And then when He's done, He returns to the table and says, *You call me Lord and master, and rightly so, for that is what I am. No servant is greater than his master* (John 13:13, 16). Boom. Mic drop. A lot of you—and this is especially true for me—don't realize that you have people above you. Superiors. Also called bosses. In our current culture, we don't like the idea of authority, so we call them peers, but the truth is "follow we" does not work. God is into leadership, and He installs leaders for a purpose.

When God establishes you as the leader, how do you respond? Do you dress yourself as a servant and do for everybody else what nobody else wants to do? Do you serve or lord it over them? At work, at school, and particularly at home, how do you live this out? Does your wife have to bug you to take out the trash, or do you just do it without being asked? How about the dishes? How about that dirty diaper?

Let me try to frame it up this way. Think of the person that you respect most in the world. An athlete, a movie star, a politician, somebody. Now imagine when you got home from work this afternoon and you hear a noise in the bathroom. You push open the door and find that person cleaning your toilet. You would say, "What are you doin'?" And they'd look at you and respond, "Somebody needs to work on their aim." To which your wife would respond with a nod. "Been talking about that for twenty years." You would feel uncomfortable. It'd be weird. You'd be like, "Oh no, you don't need to do that. You shouldn't do that."

This is what it was like for the Almighty Son of Man to get on his hands and knees and wash His disciples' feet. So what is the thing in your house, in your work, that nobody else wants to do? Do you do that thing? Jesus did. A strong man is a serving man.

The motivation behind Jesus' serving was love. Not recognition. Not false humility. Jesus sat back down and said, *I have set for you an example. You will be blessed if you do likewise* (John 13:15, 17).

A lot of people serve. Why do you serve? Some people serve out of guilt, because they still don't trust the gospel. They don't understand that they were saved by grace through faith and not by work, so they're still working to earn something. Other people serve because they're forced to. They need to let that go, and they need to serve because Christ first served us at the cross. Sometimes we serve out of pure obligation. And sometimes we serve out of manipulation. Which is especially true of us fellas. We're the worst. We serve our wives when we want something.

Am I right or is it just me? If you haven't read *The Five Love Languages*, you should. Especially men—we need it like crazy. The premise of the book is you give and receive love like a language, so you need to learn to speak your wife's love language. We should live with our wife in such a way that our life, our service of her, fills her tank. But for most of us we give to get. We just do. We're selfish sinners. We fill her tank because in reality, we want her to fill ours. That is not love, that is not service.

What kind of man are you? A serving man? A strong man? A humble man? A sabbathed man? A persevering man? Bring to mind the most important man in your life. The most influential man in your life. The most powerful man in your life. Honestly, this could be both a really good thing or a really bad thing. But bring to mind the person, the man, who has impacted you more than any other man in your entire life. They could be alive, they could be gone, whatever.

What if that man was a sabbathed man? What if he wasn't worn out, and instead of snapping at you he responded in love? And what if instead of jockeying for worldly position, he was rested and positioned at the feet of Jesus?

And what if that man that you're thinkin' about was a persevering man? What if he got up every time he got knocked down? Every single time. And what if that man stuck with you because he promised he would never ever throw in the towel? And so he never gave up on you and didn't walk away even when it was really tough. What if he stood right by you, especially when you were walking through the valley of the shadow of death? Or what if that man fought for you and not against you when you were a kid? No matter how hard it got, no matter how nasty, what if that man was a persevering man?

And what if he was a humble man? Instead of pushing you down, what if he lifted you up? Instead of cursing, what if he spoke words of life and blessing? And instead of bringing chaos into the room, what if he brought peace? What if every time you felt low, he just got a little bit lower than you so he could just pick you up and speak the words and the truth of God into your life?

And what if he was a serving man who always signed up first to take that one job nobody wanted? What if he was so patient with you because he was serving you in love? What if the most powerful man in your life was that kind of man? How different would your world be? How different would your home be? How different would your church be? Your city?

Here's the truth of this really difficult gospel—despite all your faults and failures, you can be that man. The measure of man is not power and possessions and position, but the true measure of a man is found in the person and work of Jesus Christ. I implore you to be a strong man, because a day is coming when your friends and family will dress you up, put you in a box, and bury you six feet under. The death rate is still hovering at 100 percent. Nobody escapes it. And when people gather around to talk about you, what will they talk about? Your power? Your possessions? Your position? Probably not. Will they talk about how they want to live their lives like you? Are you their model? Will they say, *You know what, he was a good man, full of the Holy Spirit and faith, and a great number of people were brought to the Lord*? Straight up, what do you want people to say about you?

Because they will. They will say something. And what they say is, in large part, up to you right now and how you live your life. Will you live like a man who lays down his life for others or who lives for himself? Those are your two options. Is your life all about you and what you want, or does your life look like that of Jesus, who became nothing so that we might live? You should stop right there and think about that. Let it sink in. The King of Kings humbled Himself. For you. For me. Never demanding anything.

What do you demand?

PRAY WITH ME

Our good and gracious heavenly Father God, we thank You so much that Jesus taught us to relate to You primarily as Father. And Lord, I know all kinds of people are reading this book. Some are really good dads, and some are really imperfect dads. And God, I thank You so much that You are not a reflection of our earthly fathers, but You are the perfection of what it means to be Father. And Father, I pray that we, Your sons and daughters, would act in the identity that You have claimed for us. That we are sons, adopted into Your family, and Your heirs, that all that You have is available to us. And God, I pray for these men. Lord, we repent of our pride. We repent of our egos. We repent of our selfishness, and by the power of the Holy Spirit, by the love of heaven, heavenly Father, by the blood of Jesus, may we live after the example set by You, the great God-man. The strongest man to ever live. And Lord, we can't do anything about our past except learn from it, and be forgiven of it. There are no second chances. And so, God, I pray that the men reading this would from this day forward be strong in the mighty hand of God. And we pray this in the good strong name of Jesus. Amen.

DOING THE STUFF

Flat-out, some of you need to serve. You need to humble yourself, go home, take out the trash, wash dishes, mop floors, whatever you don't want to do, you need to do that. You need to get your lazy behind off the couch and do that thing you expect her to do. Your wife may look at you like you've lost your mind, but you need to do it. And you need to do it today. And you need to do it the day after that. And the day after that. I'm not telling you to be a doormat but let's be honest, you're a long way from that. And don't do it because of what you might get from it, do it because you love her, because she's the most precious woman on planet Earth to you and because you want to serve her like Christ serves the church.

Some of you need to serve your kids. You need to show up at practice. You need to learn the words of their favorite Taylor Swift song. Take 'em out for a cheeseburger. Get ice cream. Take your daughter shopping for shoes she doesn't need. Take your boy fishing. Or to the range. Or something where what he wants to do is more important than your work. Kids spell love T-I-M-E, so spell it with them.

Some of you need to stop being a tyrant at work. You need to stop yelling, stop demanding. Some of you need to apologize (more than once). Some of you need to roll up your sleeves, drink coffee in the employees' break room, learn their first names and where their kids go to school, and ask them what they're dreaming. Some of you need to find out what your people are good at and let them do more of it rather than demand they do what you want. Some of you need to realize the world does not revolve around you and you need to ask your assistant, "What am I missing? How can I serve these folks better?" Trust me, she probably has her hands on the pulse of your business better than you.

And some of you need to stop chasing that white ball on Sundays and ask where you can serve the church. His bride is far more important than your handicap. It's a game. Let it go. You're not Tiger. Never will be.

Bottom line—what is that thing you don't want to do? Yes, that one. Start there.

Ready, break!

Chapter 5

LOVE IS...

If I speak in the tongues of men and of angels, but have not love, I am a noisy gong or a clanging cymbal. And if I have prophetic powers, and understand all mysteries and all knowledge, and if I have all faith, so as to remove mountains, but have not love, I am nothing. If I give away all I have, and if I deliver up my body to be burned, but have not love, I gain nothing. Love is patient and kind; love does not envy or boast; it is not arrogant or rude. It does not insist on its own way; it is not irritable or resentful; it does not rejoice at wrongdoing, but rejoices with the truth. Love bears all things, believes all things, hopes all things, endures all things. Love never ends. As for prophecies, they will pass away; as for tongues, they will cease; as for knowledge, it will pass away. For we know in part and we prophesy in part, but when the perfect comes, the partial will pass away. When I was a child, I spoke like a child, I thought like a child, I reasoned like a child. When I became a man, I gave up childish ways. For now we see in a mirror dimly, but then face to face. Now I know in part; then I shall know fully, even as I have been fully known.

> *So now faith, hope, and love abide, these three; but the greatest of these is love.*
>
> —*1 Corinthians 13:1–13*

If you've got your tissues, and all your issues, welcome to chapter 5. You're in good company. We'll be spending our time in 1 Corinthians 13, commonly known as the "love" chapter. Most everyone reads this at their wedding and then forgets about it, which is one reason why the divorce rate hovers at 50 percent. Remember, marriage is a covenant, not a contract, which means when we say, "I will" and "I do," we are covenanting before God that we will lay down our life for our wife, even when she doesn't do what we want. Even when she doesn't live up to her end of the bargain. More simply put, we are saying, "I will do, even when you don't." That's a covenant. It's also a pretty good definition of "love," but we'll get to that.

This will be a confession chapter for me. It's a doozy, so hang on. Our theme verse in this book has been 1 Corinthians 16:13–14. The center of it has been that statement "Act like men" and the imperatives around it that explain how we are to act like men. And, to be honest, I've enjoyed the writing up until now. I have a lot of confidence in being a Godly man. In being the kind of man God has called me to be. I mean, I'm not a boy that can shave. I take on responsibility. I know who God is. I know who I am in Him. I feel pretty good about that one. I'm watchful. I stand on the wall to defend my family, the people, and our church. And I understand the schemes of the enemy and what he's going to throw at me, so I'm pretty good at armoring up. And I stand firm in the faith. To stand against the schemes of the enemy. I am strong. Not just physically, but I am well aware that my strength was given to me not for me, but for my family and others.

So, I was kind of patting myself on the back until I got to verse 14, "Let all that you do be done in love." At first, I thought, *Man, I'm smoking this one too*. But then I started unpacking how the Bible defines "love," and when I compared myself to that, it didn't take me long to realize I get a big fat F on this one. My love report card reads, "Failure. Repeat grade." But before I got too down on myself, I realized I wasn't alone in this one. So if you were laughing at my expense, buckle up for the butt whooping you're about to receive. This one may sting you a little. It did me.

When Paul, inspired by the Holy Spirit, wrote his letter to the Corinthians, he didn't just pull chapter 13 out of the blue. It falls within a context. Specifically, between chapters 12 and 14. Before we get to chapter 13, Paul is talking about church leadership, how we do communion, how we have orderly worship services, and how we deal with the gifts of the Spirit. In chapter 14, he talks about unity in the church. Which centers around relationship. Taken in context, chapter 13 fits perfectly because love happens in the context of relationships. And, from what Paul says, while the Corinthian church was a very gifted church and exercised all the spiritual gifts, they were not a very loving church. Not to mention they were getting drunk at Communion. If you get drunk at Communion, you should probably start attending some meetings. You have issues.

Structurally, chapter 13 breaks into three different parts. Verses 1 through 3 talk about the necessity and promise of love, or how important it is. Verses 4 through 7 describe and apply love, and then verses 8 through 13 speak of the permanence of love. And it is here, in the permanence of love, that we find the challenge to men.

So let's pick it up. Verse 1: "If I speak in the tongues of men and of angels, but have not love, I am a noisy gong or a clanging cymbal." Again, he is saying this in the context of church leadership.

In other words, he's saying, *"If you hear the best sermons you've ever heard in your life and your pastor is preaching the paint off the walls, but it doesn't spur you to love one another, then it's all for nothing. You're just a noisy gong or a clanging cymbal."* Paul uses this noisy-gong imagery because people in Corinth would have been familiar with it, as it described much of the worship found in pagan temples. A lot of noise. Lot of chaos. A lot of sex with temple prostitutes. Not a lot of sacrificial love.

Verse 2: "And if I have prophetic powers, and understand all mysteries and all knowledge." Can you imagine having prophetic powers? Knowing the future? Understanding all mysteries. That means you'd know who shot JFK. What's really in Area 51. And never lose at *Jeopardy!* Daily Double every time. He says if you have that, "and if [you] have all faith, so as to remove mountains." Now imagine that. Not only can you predict the future, but you had so much faith that every time you prayed, *boom!* every prayer is answered. Exactly as you prayed. But Paul turns that on its head because he says you can have all that, but if you don't have love, you're nothing.

Paul is telling us here that if you accomplish everything in this world, but you do it in a loveless way and without love, then you gain nothing, and you are nothing. If you get the biggest house, and you land the dream job, and you outperform all the competition, and you shoot one under, and you buy the sweetest boat, and you impress the most people, and your YouTube video goes viral, and you pastor the fastest-growing church in America, and yet you do all that without love, then according to God, it counts for nothing and you are a complete failure.

You may ask, "Well, that seems kind of harsh, why would you say that?" Because in Matthew 22:35–39, a lawyer comes up to Jesus and says, *"Jesus, in the whole Bible, what's the most important commandment?"* The lawyer knew there were over six hundred laws to choose from, so he was trying to trick Him. That is what lawyers do. They ask you hard questions and then bill you while you work out the answers.

Jesus doesn't even flinch. *"That's easy. Love God, and love people."* Notice, "love" was the answer. Which obviously the lawyer was not doing, as he was attempting to find the loophole and weasel out. Now, the problem you and I have is that the kind of love Jesus was talking about, the kind of love that we find in 1 Corinthians 13, is called agape love, from a Greek term. Agape love is a sacrificial love. It's a me-for-you kind of love. Most often, when you and I hear the word "love," we think of the Greek word "eros." Eros is a taking kind of love. A romantic love.

When we see these words, "Let all that you do be done in love," we think about feelings and passion. We think eros. But the reality is in our world you can be the hottest couple, the richest couple, the most famous couple with a ton of passion, and if you do not have agape love, then you fail. You're nothing. See most of Hollywood for exhibit A.

Don't believe me? I don't need to name names or point fingers, but how many times have we seen the most popular couple in TV or movies and they're crushing it? Covers of all the magazines. They got money. Gorgeous good looks. Wealth. Even got good intentions. Their dinner table looks like the UN. They're bringing people together. But because they have not submitted to the Lordship of Jesus, they are not built on agape love. They have no staying power.

If you build a marriage, a covenant before God, on anything other than the love of God, your marriage will not make it. It will crash and burn. She's not always going to look like that. If you've got enough money you can tuck it, tie it up, enhance it, inject it, and stretch it back, but sooner or later, time and gravity catch up with everyone. None of us escape. And is it just me, or does gravity seem to pull on some of us a little harder than the rest of us? Maybe that's just me. Eventually, all of us are going to look like a trash bag full of water.

My definition of "love" is this: Love is your joy in the Lord expressed toward others at great expense to yourself. That's what love is. Love is your joy in the Lord expressed toward others. And that love does not happen in a vacuum. And you may ask, "Where do you get a definition like that?" I get it from Jesus Christ on the cross. His joy in the Lord expressed toward us at great expense to himself. At any moment on the cross he could have said, "That's enough, stop it." And a legion of angels would have come down and just shut the whole thing down. So every moment that He experienced suffering He had to decide and redecide and rechoose to love us by pouring Himself out on the cross. Minute by minute He did that. He chose us and He chose us and He chose us. That's different than a feeling, because I'm pretty sure He didn't feel like enduring the cross for a bunch of sinners like us. We're not worth it.

Except to Him. So, He did. He loved us.

When most of us say, "I love you," we actually mean, *I love me when I'm with you. Or when I'm around you. Or when I think of us together. And you help me love me better. That's why I love you.* Really, that means *I love me.* How can I say that? Think about it. You tell me nice things. You do nice things for me. You help me be a better version of me. Therefore, most of the time when we say, "I love you," what we really mean is, *I love the me I am when I'm around you, so why don't you hang around so we can help me love me just a little bit better?*

Is that too harsh? Sting a little too much? Stick around. It gets better.

In verse 4, we get a description and an application of love. Not what you think it is, and not what you feel like love is, but what it really is. When we started this chapter I told you this would be the confession chapter, and here it is. This is where I get an F, total and complete. And this is not me writing in some sick version of false humility so you feel better about yourself. This is me being honest when the Bible reads me. Because that's what it does when we read it. It reads us.

Here's what I mean. "Love is patient and kind." Right out of the blocks, I'm 0 for 2. Straight-up "o-fer." No one that I know has ever used those words to describe me. Tim Tebow? Yes. My wife, Gretchen? Definitely. Dr. Piper? Absolutely. Joby Martin? Eh…not so much.

Truth is, I am impatient. A lot. When I get behind the wheel of my truck, I feel like everybody in front of me is beating me, or purposefully trying to get in my way just to slow me down. Don't they know I've got people to see? Places to go? Like, to football practice.

The other day I was returning south down I-95, heading to my son's practice, when an officer pulled me over. So help me, I was not paying attention. My mind was focused anywhere but on my speed, but obviously, subconsciously, I was doing my little impatient thing. His lights flashed, and I pulled over and rolled down my window. He said, "Sir, you know I clocked you at 93 mph?" Honestly, no. I didn't. But, the point is I was and he did. That's the truth of me. I just shook my head. "My bad. Do what you got to do."

Truth is, in my heart of hearts, more often than not, I'm focused on me. Not those around me. Reminds me of Paul when he says in Romans 7, *There is a sin that dwells in me.* 'Cause there is. Can I get a witness? When I told Gretchen about the speeding ticket, she was like, "Why you gotta pass everybody?"

"'Cause they're in front of me. I don't worry about them when they're behind me."

Patience is the passive reaction of love to tough circumstances in people. Literally, in Greek, "patience" means to "take a punch."

When I think, *I can take a punch*, it's usually the setup for me to punch back. But if we are going to follow Jesus, there's no counterpunch to our circumstances. And patience and kindness go together. Kindness is the active action toward those people who are requiring your patience. Love is both of those. Patient and kind.

Back to my scorecard—I'm still o-fer: 0 for 2. And it gets worse. "Love does not envy or boast." Here I'm fifty-fifty: 1 and 1. I don't envy, but I can and do boast. Just listen to me talk about hunting, and pretty soon my phone's coming out and so are the pictures. So, I boast all the time, but I'm totally okay with who God has created me to be and I feel like the most blessed man in the world. I'm not really envious of other people's stuff or position.

When looking at the word "envy," several translations say, "Love is not jealous." Which can be confusing, because the Bible also says that God is love and that God is a jealous God. So what does it mean? It means that love is jealous *for* but not jealous *of*. Big difference. It means God is jealous for you. Not jealous of you. Which would be silly. It'd be like God looking at you and saying, "Those are some sweet pants. I wish I had pants like that."

What do you possess that God could possibly look at and want? Nothing. Why? Because He made everything. He's not looking at you to supply His needs. You think He looks at your granite countertops and wishes he had those in His bathroom, when He created granite? Saying He's jealous for you means He wants the best for you. He knows that if you choose to worship anything or any god other than Him, it does not go good for you. In fact, that'd be the worst thing for you. So, He's jealous for you in a way that wants the absolute best for you.

So back to love. First Corinthians 13:4 says, *Love is patient. Love is kind. It does not envy or boast. It is not arrogant or rude.* Are you arrogant and rude? I am, more often than I like to admit. Arrogance makes you think that you're actually better than everybody else, and rudeness makes you treat them that way. Ask yourself this: When you walk in the room, or a house, or an office, or any place with other people, do you act like God put them on this earth to serve you? Do you think He placed them in your life so that you could accomplish all the great things you set out to accomplish? Do you look at them as supporting cast in the epic adventure of you? If the answer to this is yes, then chances are about 100 percent you're arrogant. And let me be the first to raise my hand here—I'm guilty of this. I am so guilty of this.

Here's how you know if you're also guilty: When you walk in the door, does peace walk in with you? Do those around you know that you have come in to serve or to be served? Love is not arrogant or rude and does not insist on its own way. Do you have to have your own way? Do you manipulate people to get your own way? How about passive manipulation? Do you always have to have the last word? This is another area where I'm a wretched, black-hearted sinner. You can ask Gretchen. She asks me this all the time. When we're having moments of intense fellowship, she asks, "Why do you always have to be right?" To which I think, *Who wants to be wrong? Why don't you just cross on over to my side, and we'll both be right together, and then it will all be awesome?*

And to make matters worse, I know the Bible pretty well and I can usually support my need to be right with some verse that I bend to support my rightness. But love doesn't do that. Love is not irritable or resentful. The NIV translates that word "irritable" as "easily angered" in verse 5. Are you easily angered? Does the slightest little thing set you off? Be honest. Look into the mirror and ask yourself, "Is that me?" When you walk in your house, do your family members think, *Uh-oh, he's home. Who do we get today? Hope he's in a good mood.*

One of the things you're gonna find in 1 Corinthians 13 is an absence of excuses to not be loving. Here's the inexcusable truth about all of us—we're all just like Adam. "It's not my fault. I'm tired, I'm stressed. She did it. Don't look at me." Our heart problem has got nothing to do with her and everything to do with us. If I'm gut-level honest, I'm irritable because I didn't get my way, or I'm bracing myself because I know I'm about to not get my way. Which at its root is unloving. Act that way long enough, and you will become resentful, and resentment is harboring unforgiveness with this low-grade disappointment because you didn't get what you wanted. You wake up, and your face looks like you were weaned on a pickle. You walk into the kitchen and your wife asks, "You okay?"

You're irritated by the question, but you manage, "Yes, why?"

To which she responds, "You should tell your face."

I'm guilty as charged. Gretchen says this to me all the time. I am the world's worst at this.

Listen, you who call yourself a man, I dare you. I dare you to ask the people that work for you or your family, "What is it like to be on the other side of me?" The reality is if you're irritable and resentful, they probably won't tell you the truth because they don't want to deal with the whirlwind that follows. But what if you gave them permission without the wrath? The kind of environment where they can tell you the truth about you without fear of blowback or retribution? Ask your wife. Your kids. Your coworkers. Then listen for the response. Their words might surprise you.

Verse 6: "[Love] does not rejoice at wrongdoing, but rejoices with the truth." Again, I grew up on the NIV and it's what I memorized first. That's not to say it's the best translation. It's not. But sometimes I like the way it phrases things. Like this one. The NIV translates verse 5 as "[Love] keeps no record of wrongs." Bingo. That one hits me like a ton of bricks. You catch me on a bad day and I've got a deck of IOUs in my back pocket. Anybody else? Am I alone in this one? Doubtful. Men, are you keeping score? Do you keep a scorecard on everybody? Are you counting the last time she was sweet to you? When you got what you wanted? And then are you underlining all the times you didn't? When she said she was tired?

You know what a lot of us do? We keep a ledger, a running scorecard on everybody else, so that we can build a case for future argument. We're stacking the deck in our favor so that when we're confronted for our bad, or unloving, behavior, we can counter their argument with the number of times they did the exact same thing to us. "See, I'm not the only one. You did this to me. Umpteen times." That's great if you're a lawyer, not so much if you're a husband, boss, or father. Love does not do that. Love forgives. Love keeps no record.

If you've ever studied how other people fight, you'll recognize how quickly some get hysterical. Throwing haymakers. I get historical. I can dredge up every time somebody dinged me. "Yeah, you remember back in 2001, it was a Thursday night, you did that thing…" The Bible says—it commands—no, don't do that.

The Greek word for this phrase is "logizomai." "Logos" is Greek for "word." That means that love does not talk about or continuously bring up others' wrongs. Love forgives. Love doesn't even talk about the times it's been treated badly. It doesn't give those events any power. Right this minute, there are a whole bunch of relationships that are handcuffed in the future because they're stuck in the past and what happened. Why? Because you won't forgive, and you keep bringing out that IOU from your pocket. Love rejoices in the truth. Do you? Do you spend more time pointing out the negatives in everybody's life than praising the positives? Here's an easy litmus test: Scroll through the last week of texts to your wife, employees, and children, and count them. Was what you said negative or a comment on how they could have done something better, or was it positive, encouraging, praising what they had done or what God had done in and through them?

According to the Bible, the opposite of love is not hate. It's selfishness. Love says, "It's not about me." Selfishness says, "It's all about me." "Love bears all things, believes all things, hopes all things, endures all things" (1 Cor. 13:7). In other words, love never quits. Not ever.

Let me get real practical. Husbands, this means you never give up pursuing the heart of your wife. You could be in the middle of an ugly divorce—which is probably your fault—but it's not too late. Don't give up. And you don't let your past define you. You might have been that man at one time, but you don't have to be him right now or ever again. You can be a Godly man and fight for the heart of your wife. Even if she's already left you, and even if she's already filed papers. Those papers do not tell you who you are. Jesus tells you who you are. Some court decision does not define your marriage. God defines your marriage. Some of you are thinking, *Gosh, I'm in an impossible situation*. You probably are, but if Jesus' tomb is empty, anything is possible.

Also, do not give up fighting for the hearts of your children. Especially when they're teenagers. Their plan is to wear you down. It's what they spend half their time Snapchatting about. Despite their rebellion, what they wear matters. Where they go matters. Who they're with matters. It doesn't matter if they like you. Matter of fact, it's not your job to make your kids like you. If you love them, you—in your wisdom, age, and stage of life—are going to make decisions for them that they will not like. Such as curfews. But we all know nothing good happens after midnight. And if you're divorced, your battle is not against flesh and blood. Your battle is not against your ex. Pray for unity with your ex so that both of you can fight as one for the hearts of your children.

Here's the goal—when they become adults, and they're looking back on their lives, they should know their daddy never quit fighting for them. He never gave up. Never tapped out. Some of you are thinking, *Have you met my kids?* Jesus knows your kids. He created them. Loves them more than you do. And His response is, *"Love bears all things, and love believes all things, and love hopes all things, and love endures all things"* (v. 7). And if His tomb is empty, then anything is possible, because love is alive and is found in Jesus Christ.

Now that we've made it through the beatdown, let me ask you—and be honest—how're you doing? Do any of you want to raise your hand and say, *Nailing it. Just crushing it. Wish Paul would've thrown in a couple others 'cause this is kindergarten stuff.* Anybody there? If you say yes, then you're boasting, which makes you both a liar and a hypocrite.

A few days ago, I spent the morning in the woods up at our retreat center marinating on all this. After a quick look in the mirror, things were not good. I called Gretchen on the way home and said, "Babe, I owe you an apology."

This caught her off guard because I don't usually begin conversations this way. "What's wrong?"

I said, "You know I love you, but I have not been loving you. And you know I love our children, but I have not been loving our children. I have been more unloving than loving. I'm sorry. I don't want to be like that."

This got her attention, so she said, "Can we talk about this when you get home?"

I got home, and she could tell I was really ruffled, and she said, "What do you mean?"

I tried to explain and she cut me off, "No, baby, you love us. We're so blessed. You love our kids. You love me. I love you. We're good."

To which I said, "Well, okay, let's just look through the list here and, and you tell me how I'm doing?"

She quickly scanned the list, kind of tilted her head, and patted my thigh. "Babe, I'll be praying for you."

Gretchen knows as well as I do that I don't measure up very well when the measuring line is 1 Corinthians 13. I fail miserably. I'm not patient or kind. I boast a lot. I'm arrogant, rude, and I always have to have my own way. I'm irritable and resentful, and I keep a long record of wrongs committed against me. I do a pretty good job of hiding these things, but I still do them.

And to make matters worse for me, the chapter doesn't end there. It continues in verses 8–10, where it says, "Love never ends." And the reason it never ends is because God is love and God never ends. "As for prophecies, they will pass away; as for tongues, they will cease; as for knowledge, it will pass away. For we know in part and we prophesy in part, but when the perfect comes, the partial will pass away."

In other words, here on earth, all these things are important—prophecies, tongues, words of knowledge—but we will have zero need for them in heaven. Why? Because we will be coheirs with God. He will share everything with us. Everything He has is yours and mine. It'll be like being on vacation with your dad. You can walk into His throne room and ask him yourself. "Hey Dad?"

"Yeah, son."

Think of it this way: There will be no more sermons in heaven. Why will we need anyone like me to help you understand His Word when the living Word will be there speaking to us and with us? Face-to-face. It's not like we're going to be gathered with God, Jesus, and the Holy Spirit—one God in three persons—all sitting on the throne of glory, however that works, while the elders around Him bow down and cast their crowns at His feet, saying, "Holy, holy,

holy, it's the Lord God Almighty who was and is, and is to come." All while myriads upon myriads, or hundreds of millions of angels, sing in perfect unison around them, only to be interrupted as the PA system crackles, "Uh, attention all of heaven. Pastor Joby Martin of Jacksonville, Florida, from the second millennium, will be doing a series on Ephesians in Room 316 starting in fifteen minutes. Get there early to make sure you get a seat."

It's just not happening. I mean, seriously, what would I say? "Okay, um, if you've got your Bible, go to Ephesians. While you're turning there I want to take a minute and recognize Paul...Hey, Paul, good to see you. Thanks for being here. Looking forward to your contribution. I'd also like to welcome the Ephesians. What's up, guys? Welcome. Glad you're here."

Nope. Those days are over. But the thing that will remain is the love of God. And then, right in here in the eternity of love, we get this command: "When I was a child, I spoke like a child, I thought like a child, I reasoned like a child. When I became a man, I gave up childish ways" (v. 11).

What are childish ways? Everything love is not. To be honest, I've never seen it this way before, and I read my Bible a lot. It's a challenge. Paul's saying, *When I was a baby, I wasn't very patient and kind. And when I was a baby, I was jealous of what everybody else had, and I bragged about everything I had. And when I was a baby, I was arrogant and rude. I thought the whole world revolved around me. And when I was a baby, I had to constantly have my own way, and I was irritable and resentful.*

Think about it. Is anybody more selfish than a child? And I know you think your little snowflake is precious but be honest for a second. They're a selfish little snowflake. Have you ever met a patient child? Children are naturally rude and arrogant, and they think the whole world revolves around them. You ever been in a restaurant sitting next to a baby screaming its head off? You ever been in an airplane when somebody's kid flops down in the middle of the aisle and throws a feet-kicking, arm-swinging tantrum? If it's been a minute since you've hung around young kids, do yourself a favor and hang out on the cereal aisle at Publix this afternoon when the moms bring the kids through after school. Watch what happens when the children don't get the cereal they want. Or when a kid misses a nap. Or they take away their children's toys.

Paul is saying, *Yeah, me too. When I was a baby, I cried like a baby and I pooped all over myself as a baby, but when I became a man I put away my sippy cup, my passy, and my blanky* (v. 11).

Men, let's call it straight—we have a problem, and the problem is us. We're loud, obnoxious, throwing tantrums and walking around in diapers that should have been changed years ago and are full of warm, squishy, smelly stuff. Truth is, we kind of like sitting in it 'cause it's ours. We're selfish, we've constantly got to have our own way, we flex our strength and our authority and our manhood and make everything about us. Then, just to make sure everyone knows how great we are, we boast and pound our chests and demand those around us serve us. We're unkind to those around us and beneath us. We're impatient, and we bark orders like the world owes us something. We think we are being tough. Paul says that we are acting like toddlers.

Just this week, we were having trouble with our propane tank. Gretchen called the gas company three times and they didn't call her back. I said, "Give me the number." So I called them, barked at them, told them to get out there and fix our tank or they could come pick it up off the curb. Which is ridiculous. The thing weighs four hundred pounds. I couldn't lift it even on my best day. I'd drop it, blow up the whole neighborhood, and we'd be in the news. It's not even possible. But that didn't stop me. I just needed to rattle my sword cause I'm thinking, *I'm the man.*

This is not at all how Jesus would have called the gas company.

Truth is, when we try to act tough, we're not being tough. We're being a toddler. Straight up, you want to be a man? Love the unlovable. That's what Paul's saying. James 4:1 says, "What causes fights and quarrels among you?" (NIV). In other words, why are you pitching a fit? To which we respond with a list of excuses. But James is very practical. You want to know why James is very practical? Because James was the brother of Jesus. How would you like to grow up with a perfect brother? Think about it. Not easy. Your parents would be saying, "Why can't you be more like your brother?"

James asks, "What causes fights and quarrels among you?" Why are you so irritable? Why are you pitching a fit? And then he answers his own question. It's really quite simple—because you want something, and when you don't get it, you revert to being a child.

If you are to stand firm and act like a man, you will put these childish ways behind you. You will be patient. Kind. Not envious. You won't boast.

Then we get to 1 Corinthians 13:12, which says, "For now we see in a mirror dimly, but then face to face. Now I know in part; then I shall know fully, even as I have been fully known." Due to the Fall, we don't see God, ourselves, or each other, the way God intends. Sin has fogged our lens. One day, when we are with Jesus in our glorified bodies, we will give and receive love perfectly and without hindrance. Until then, we've got work to do.

Verse 13: "So now faith, hope, and love abide." These three are really big deals. Faith is the currency by which we know God. Hebrews 11:6 says, "Without faith it is impossible to please him [God]." Faith, trust, and belief are all the same word. The way that we have a relationship with God is putting our faith in Jesus Christ, that we are saved by grace through faith. It is the vehicle by which God's grace is poured out on us. Faith is a really big deal, and yet there is no faith in heaven. We won't need it. Nobody's going to come up to you in heaven and ask, "Do you believe in Jesus?" There's no need. He's sitting right there. Shining like ten trillion suns. You can just ask him.

There is also no hope in heaven. On earth right now, we need hope. It's the fuel that feeds us. Gets us to the finish line. The Bible says that hope deferred makes the heart sick. I'd rather have a sick body than a sick heart. Hope deferred makes the heart sick, and in that same Book of Proverbs, it says above all else, guard your heart for it is the wellspring of life. It's really important to have hope in your heart. When you lose hope, you feel helpless, and the whole world goes dark on you. So is hope important? Absolutely. Here on earth. But there's no hope in heaven because the things that we are hoping for we will experience firsthand every day. We will no longer need to hope for perfect love because we will be living eternally in its presence.

"So now faith, hope, and love abide, these three; but the greatest of these is love" (1 Cor. 13:13). Love matters for eternity. My definition again is this: Love is your joy in the Lord expressed toward others at great expense to yourself. You should let that sink in—your joy in the Lord expressed toward others at great expense to yourself.

Which begs the question—and you knew it was coming—how are you doing? Are you loving? Now, if at this moment you don't think, *I should be more loving*, then I'm not doing a very good job telling you what the Bible says about love. Also, if you put down this book, return to your life, and just try harder, you'll fail miserably. Sorry to break it to you, but you don't have it in you to love well. You will be trying to give something to others that you don't have in you. How do I know? Because if you did have it in you, you would have done it by now. But you haven't because you don't.

Absent Jesus, you can't love anyone. He is the source of love, so unless you're drawing from the source, your well is dry. I'm going to run through a bunch of verses to help explain this. First John 4:7–8 starts out this way: "Beloved, let us love one another, for love is from God, and whoever loves has been born of God and knows God. Anyone who does not love does not know God."

Even if you know your Bible and can quote a hundred verses, and even if you've been doing the church thing a minute, and even when I told you to go to 1 Corinthians 13 you thought *Love chapter*, and even if you've led a dozen mission trips, and even if you know the words to every worship song, and you worship with your eyes closed and one hand up, and even if you do all this and more, and yet you don't know love, then you don't know God. Why? Because God is love. God, in and of Himself, is in a perfect love relationship. This theology matters a lot. The triune God, Father, Son, and Spirit, one God in three persons, live in a perfect, submissive love relationship with one another. And why does that matter? Because God's love for God's self spilled out into creation. Creation did not occur because God was slipping through the ether one evening and thought to Himself, *What are we going to do with all this space and time? We need some people who will sing us songs on the weekend and then disobey me all week.* This was not how it worked.

God's love for Himself spills out, and He creates humankind in His image and likeness. Which is why we humans are the only created things with the ability to love, because we were the only ones created in His image and likeness. What does this mean? I hate to break it to you, but it means your dog does not love you. I know you love your dog, but your dog does not love you back. Your dog loves bacon and if you died in your apartment tonight, he would eat your neck meat to stay alive. Think about that next time you feed him.

First John 4:19 says, "We love because he first loved us." This means the only reason we are capable of love is because God is love and when His love is in us, we can be a conduit for that love. His love fills us up and overflows out of us and toward others, but it doesn't originate in us. We don't have love in and of ourselves. We have emotion and passion, but we are not capable of sacrificial love absent Jesus in us. Jesus says in John 15:13–14, "Greater love has no one than this, that someone lay down his life for his friends. You are my friends if you do what I command you." Then He went to the cross and laid His life down for us. Which is the model for how we're supposed to love one another. At great expense to ourselves.

Romans 5:8 says, "But God shows his love for us in that while we were still sinners, Christ died for us." This means God is first, God loved first, and God went first. That does not mean that God waits until I get a passing grade on the love test in 1 Corinthians 13 before He loves me. His love for us is not conditional on our performance. He loves us because He loves us. Period. Doing something or not doing something doesn't change that.

First John 4:10 tells us, "In this is love, not that we have loved God, but that he loved us and sent his son to be a propitiation for our sin." Propitiation means a payment that satisfies. When Christ died on the cross, He atoned for our sin and satisfied the righteous requirement of the law. So what's crazy is that not only are our sins forgiven, but we also get credit for His righteous, perfect life.

Think of it this way: Say you got on your smartphone right now and checked your bank account, and the balance was negative ten trillion. You'd think to yourself, *Oh, no, I am $10 trillion in debt. I'll never to be able to repay that.* I know you can't imagine such a debt, but just try. You know for certain that you don't have enough life left in you to ever pay that off. And then God comes into your little personal budget meeting here and says, "Tell you what, I'll make a deal with you. I'll take your debt and I'll give you my bank account.

Not only that, I'm going to give you the bank." How many of us would make that deal?

And then just to make sure, you check your bank account app and find more zeroes next to your name than you can count. What? How does that happen? What did you do to deserve that? God not only pays your debt but gives you access to everything that's His. C. S. Lewis called it "the Great Exchange." When Christ died on the cross, he was the propitiation for your and my sins. Not only did He pay your debt, but God, in His mercy, credited us with His righteousness. Which makes zero sense outside the inconceivable love of God.

When I called Gretchen and said, "Baby, I am failing. I am not loving you well," it was conviction and not condemnation that made me want to call her. Condemnation looks at a thing and says, "That is unfit for use." If you condemn a building, no one gets to live there. But that's not the way God looks at us. He looks at this tattered, broken building and says, "I'm gonna make that my temple. He or she is gonna be my permanent address here on earth." Crazy, right? When we surrender to the Lordship of Jesus Christ, and His Spirit fills us, the love of God has officially been poured out into my heart, which means I can now start to love as He loves us.

A great way to read 1 Corinthians 13 in a devotional way is to just put your name everywhere it says "Love" and then ask yourself how you're doing. For example, "Joby is patient and kind." Nope. "Joby does not envy or boast." Nope. "Joby is not arrogant or rude." Nope. When I read this, I feel like I hear the *Jeopardy!* buzzer going off in my ear after every one.

But here's the good news. In 1 John 4:8 we read that God is love. So now, replace your name with God's. God is patient and kind, and God does not envy or boast, and God is not arrogant or rude, and God does not insist on his own way. In fact, He stepped out of the glory of heaven and came to earth to die for sins that were not his fault. Would you sign up for that? No, because you're not love. He is. What's more, He's not irritable, not resentful, and He doesn't rejoice at wrongdoing. God keeps no record of wrongs. Some of you need to let that sink in. God is not walking the halls of heaven with a scorecard in His back pocket. "Well, Joby scored a triple bogey on that hole." The truth of Jesus is this: If you place your trust in Him, believing that He is who the Bible says He is and that He did what the Bible says He did, then He takes your record of wrongs and nails it to the cross. First Corinthians 13 is not just a test for how we're doing. All of us have failed that test ten thousand times over. First Corinthians 13 is the example of how God has loved and still loves every single one of us.

Have you ever experienced a love like that? Only when that love begins to dwell in you and invade you can you actually love like the man that you are called to be.

Here's the point: Your passivity is really just you holding back your strength and your manhood for self-preservation. You think to yourself, either consciously or unconsciously, *That looks too hard for my own comfort, so I'm not gonna get involved. I'm just going to let them ride that out.*

On the opposite end of the spectrum, aggression is expressing your strength and your manhood for self-gratification. *I'll take what I want when I want and I don't need anyone's permission.*

The problem is that both extremes are childish behavior. Quit being a child, and act like a man. If you want to love like Jesus, you will leverage your strength for others at great expense to yourself. Exactly like Christ did on the cross. Have you ever experienced a love like that? Have you ever expressed a love like that? Do you want to?

PRAY WITH ME

Our good and gracious heavenly Father, God, we love You because You first loved us. God, we thank You that You are first. And God, I thank You that Jesus came not to just be an example or a model for us to mimic, but He came to pay that debt, to give us the credit for His righteous life, and that when we surrender to You, the love of God dwells inside of us, and love never fails because You never fail. God, I repent for every way in which I am or have been unloving. Forgive me, please. Forgive me for not loving my wife, my kids, my friends, and those folks at work or on the highway. Please remove all the clutter in my life that is keeping the fruit of the spirit from bearing the fruit of love in my life. Please help me love as You love. I thank You that we can love because You first loved us. And we pray this in Jesus' name. Amen.

DOING THE STUFF

Stand up. Right where you are. Stand firm. Align yourself for battle. Act like a man. And in order to act like a man of God, do two things daily: Kneel before the King, and lay down your life for those He's given you to love and serve.

Here is my question to you in this moment: How can you lay down your life for those you love? How can you serve them? How can you make their stuff more important than your stuff? Not just today, but tomorrow and the next day.

That thing that just came to your mind that you don't want to do? Go do that.

Ready, break!

Chapter 6

ARE YOU READY TO STAND FIRM AND ACT LIKE A MAN?

Now as they were eating, Jesus took bread, and after blessing it broke it and gave it to the disciples, and said, "Take, eat; this is my body." And he took a cup, and when he had given thanks he gave it to them, saying, "Drink of it, all of you, for this is my blood of the covenant, which is poured out for many for the forgiveness of sins. I tell you I will not drink again of this fruit of the vine until that day when I drink it new with you in my Father's kingdom."

—*Matthew 26:26–29*

When he had washed their feet and put on his outer garments and resumed his place, he said to them, "Do you understand what I have done to you? You call me Teacher and Lord, and you are right, for so I am. If I then, your Lord and Teacher, have washed your feet, you also ought to wash one another's feet. For I have given you an example, that you also should do just as I have done to you. Truly, truly, I say to you, a servant is not greater than his master,

> *nor is a messenger greater than the one who sent him. If you know these things, blessed are you if you do them."*
>
> —John 13:12–17

I want to circle back to something we talked about earlier. If I was your football coach, this'd be the time-out speech I'd give you with a minute left in the fourth, when we still needed to march the length of the field to win.

For all of you that, like me, are kind of thick-headed and need reminding, this is for you. Yes, you. I'm talking directly to you. Not the guy next to you, not your father-in-law, not your coworker, not those sinners in your Saturday foursome, but you. But before you think you've got to man up, put the team on your shoulders, and become the GOAT, you don't. This is not that talk. This game has already been won, so stick with me.

Remember when your kid took their first steps? I know all you young superdads posted it on YouTube using four camera angles, including slow-mo, but back in the day, we had to be present in the moment and experience it firsthand. It was unbelievable. You remember what happened? Your kid was crawling around, wrecking everything within arms' length, so you moved everything up a shelf, beyond their reach. But then they began using the shelves and chairs to pull themselves up and they started to do that whole weeble-wobble thing, but now they could reach higher, so all the stuff went up another shelf. Then, one day, they were holding on to the TV tray like a drunken sailor, hips swaying side to side, and you saw it in their eyes. They wanted the thing that was on the sofa, but that would involve falling down, crawling over, and then climbing up. Which was getting kind of old. Plus, it was going to squish whatever was in their diaper and that was getting kind of old, too. And have you ever noticed how big a baby's head is compared to the rest of its body? That big ole fat thing is huge. It's enormous. And once it gets going, gravity and momentum just take over. So, there it is. That shiny thing on the sofa and they want it so they can put it in their mouth, so they weeble-wobble, lean their head in that direction, and there's just too much momentum to stop. And right here they face a choice. Probably more unconscious than conscious, but it was a choice nonetheless. They could either face-plant, which they know from prior experience is not a whole lot of fun, or they could move one of those two things they were standing on. And so, for the first time in their life, they put one in front of the other.

And you saw it happen. They took a step. Followed by another and another. Before finally crashing into the side of the sofa. And when it happened, you called everybody you knew. "I think he's gonna be a running back 'cause he kind of made the Heisman pose right before he fell." Then and now, we celebrate every step with loud applause. When your uncle Josh does that you call him a drunk, but your baby does it and you're signing him up for gifted classes.

Here's why I bring this up. That inexplicable elation, that joy in a dad's face that just does not make sense, that ear-to-ear grin for something as mundane as a single step, is exactly how God the Father sees you. I'm serious. Regardless of what you went through last night, or what you did last week, last month, or last year, or plan on doing tomorrow, your heavenly Father is proud of you if you are in Christ. And He's crazy in love with you. Why? How can I say that? Because if you've surrendered to the Lordship of Jesus Christ, He has put His love through Jesus Christ on you. So when He looks at you, He sees the sinless, spotless, righteous life of His Son—with whom He is well pleased. Which, because of the imputed righteousness of Christ, is the way He sees you. In theological terms we call this "justified." Think of it this way—because of His Son, Jesus, God the Father sees you "just as if you'd never sinned."

So let me ask you: How do you see yourself in relation to God the Father? Do you see yourself as a bond servant or as a son? Slave or heir? Here's the thing—a bond servant's standing in the household is based on performance, how well they perform their chores. Do them well, and you're accepted and you get to work another day. Don't do them well and you're sold.

But a son? A son's standing in the home is based on position. Period. That man is my dad. I am his son. A bond servant has to pay back a debt. A son receives an inheritance. In the first century, being a bond servant was a temporary condition, or servitude, based on a contract. Labor for hire. People sold themselves into slavery, and when they had worked off their debt, they were free to go.

Sons have no debt, and sonship is forever. Sonship is bestowed. Given. Not earned. And they can't lose it. If you live with a bond servant mentality, then you just think God wants good works from you, and if you perform them you get to stay in His good graces. But when you know God as your father and you live as His son, you get to rest in His presence without the expectation of performance. Now, from that place, that standing, you might work in the Father's kingdom. There's a lot of work to be done. But make no mistake, that work is freely performed out of love-based obedience, not an obligation. Big difference.

In Luke 11:11–13, Jesus says, "What father among you, if his son asks for a fish, will instead of a fish give him a serpent; or if he asks for an egg, will give him a scorpion? If you then, who are evil, know how to give good gifts to your children, how much more will the heavenly Father give the Holy Spirit to those who ask him!" Jesus is trying to explain to a bunch of thick-headed people like us that if we, who are evil and fleshly, can give good gifts to our kids, how much more does the heavenly Father want to give us good gifts? And that good gift is the Holy Spirit.

Years ago, I was yelling at one of my kids. I only have two, so you can probably guess who it was. He had done something dumb and screwed up. I was making sure he understood that. So, in a rather loud voice, I said, "Listen to me, if you would just do what I tell you to do, your whole life would be better." And my kid looks at me and the Spirit of God was like, "Tell him again, Dad." So, I did. A little louder this time. "If you would just listen to the words I tell you…" And the Spirit of God prompted me again just to make sure he heard me the first two times. I think this time I might have even pointed. "If you would just listen…"

That's when it hit me. "Okay, wait a minute, I don't think we're talking about him anymore." To which the Spirit of God said, "You think?"

Every single time we trust Him as a son trusts his dad, we're taking steps of obedience in the direction of abundant life, because that's what He wants for us, not from us. You need to let that distinction settle in your heart. He wants *for* us, not *from* us. Every single time we do what our heavenly Father tells us to do, especially in the places where we think we know better, like sex and money and forgiveness, we are living like sons and not slaves.

In Galatians 4:6, Paul writes, "And because you are sons…" Notice he says nothing about your feelings. He is stating what you are, not what you feel like.

"Well," you might say, "I don't feel like a son." It doesn't matter. If you've placed your faith in Jesus, you are, whether you feel like it or not. Truth is, a lot of days you won't feel like a son. But I'm hammering the verse in hopes your feelings will catch up with the reality that what Christ did on the cross was enough for you, and in so doing, He returned you to the Father and gave you the right to become a child of God. None of which is earned. It's given. Your job is to believe it, receive it, and rest in it. To suggest otherwise is to despise the cross of Jesus. To trust your feelings and not His word is to stand next to the cross of Jesus, look up at his nail-pierced hands and feet and see the hole in His side, and shake your head, "Nope. Nice try but not good enough." I know you would never say that, yet sometimes we do say that by the way we live our lives. "And because you are sons, God has sent the Spirit of his Son into our hearts, crying, 'Abba! Father!'"

God is not a tyrant judge demanding obedience. If He was, He would have required our death on that cross. Instead, He did for us what we could never do for ourselves—sent His Son to die in our place. Think about that. He is a father who wants to be loved. And so when you trust Christ as your Savior, God puts a deposit of the Holy Spirit into you, and because of that we can honestly say, "Abba! Father!"

When JP was little, I'd walk in the door and he'd run around the corner, arms up, screaming, "Daddy!" Now, he's eighteen and trains in MMA, so if he reaches out, you got to guard your neck or you'll be unconscious. But I never trained him to do that arms-up-reaching-for-me-thing. That bubbled up out of his heart for me.

When we worship with our hands raised, we are doing the exact same thing. Verse 7 says this: "So you are no longer a slave, but a son, and if a son, then an heir through God." Here's what this means, and it's very technical, so listen up—what Jesus does from the cross to the resurrection, legally, actually, and objectively adopts you into God's family. But God wants more than that, so He sends the Spirit of God to live inside of you so that you may emotionally and relationally experience the reality of what Jesus legally and actually did for you. So that we wouldn't have an orphan mentality, but a sonship mentality. So that when we screw up we can run to Him and not from Him. I think if more of us understood this, we would stand in churches where every man had his hands in the air and not stuffed in his pockets.

ARE YOU READY TO STAND FIRM AND ACT LIKE A MAN?

Earlier in this book, I told you, "The most important thing about you is what you think when you think about God." So what do you think when you think about God? Do you think He's a loving heavenly Father that sings and dances over His children? Or do you think He's some kind of distant judge and He's more than just a little bit frustrated with you right now because you're annoying? The two most important things in your whole lived experience are who God is and who you are. And if you are "in Christ," then God is your Father and you are His son. But, if you're not "in Christ," then the devil is your father, and hell is hot and forever is a really long time. Sorry to have to break that to you. If you think God is just a distant creator, at best you're agnostic, and you'll think He's some uncaring force out there and you'll have no reason to want to get to Him. If you think He's an angry judge, you're going to think it's all performance and no grace. If you think He's the sky fairy that just wants you to be happy, you're going to think it's all grace and feelings, so you can do whatever you want.

If you think He's the old man upstairs and out of touch with life and reality, you will sit in judgment over His precepts. If you think He's just a ritualistic deity, then you're going to try to jump through a bunch of religious hoops looking for the right combination to appease Him. But when you know Him as Father, everything changes. And Father is not just an illustration that the Bible uses to describe who God is. God is actually our Father. It's just who He is. In the four gospels, Matthew, Mark, Luke, and John, Jesus calls the God of the universe "Father" 189 times. This was very unique. The Hebrew word for "father" is used about fifteen times in the Old Testament, and it was always used to describe God as a father of a nation. But in the New Testament, "father" is a personal word.

Listen, I get it. For some of you, it's very hard to understand who God is because your earthly dad was not the best father. When you think of a father, your dad comes to mind and it's just tough to rearrange those memories or separate them from the God of the universe. But here's the thing you need to wrap your head around—God Almighty is not a reflection of your earthly father. He is the perfection of what it means to be Father. That's why the wounds cut so deep. Think about this, in John 3:16, the most famous verse in the Bible, *For God so loved the world that He sent His only begotten Son*. We've heard this so much it's lost some of its punch, but stop and think: If you have a son, would you give him in place of anyone else on planet Earth?

That is exactly what God the Father did for you and me. Now, ask yourself, what kind of dad does that? Then look at Jesus' baptism—what happens? Jesus has lived a private family life for thirty years. He hasn't done any ministry yet, and yet the heavens cracked open and God established that He was the Father to His Son Jesus, and He said, *Behold My Son in whom I'm well pleased* (Matt. 3:17). This occurred before Jesus performed a single recorded miracle. Before He taught His first sermon. Before He ever redeemed the world. So, the Father was not pleased because of Jesus' performance. He hadn't performed yet. The Father was simply pleased with His Son because He was His Son. And because Jesus was a son, He was loved by His dad.

When Jesus' disciples came up to Him in Luke 11 and they asked, "Lord, teach us to pray," Jesus made it really simple. He started it this way: "Our Father..." To which the disciples scratched their heads. They must have been thinking, *What? Don't you mean "creator," "judge," "sovereign"?*

It's true. He is all of those things. No doubt. But He—God Almighty, the Lord of Hosts—primarily wants you to know that He is our Father. And the reason that we can pray is because of what Christ does on the cross. When Jesus goes on to the cross and pushes up on His nail-pierced feet and says, "It is finished," an earthquake cracks right through the middle of Jerusalem, right through the temple, and it tears the curtain that separated the people of God from the presence of God from the top to the bottom. That was God's invitation for His children. You don't have to kill a goat and talk to a priest anymore in order to commune with God because now, if you believe in Christ, you're His kid. And if you're the kid of the king, then you're the only person in the empire who could just walk into the king's chambers at three o'clock in the morning and wake up the king and say, "Hey, Daddy, can I get a drink?"

If you're a parent, do you remember when your little kid had those terrible dreams at night? I know you felt you were being stalked by a zombie, but you'd open your eyes and your toddler would be right there looking at you and he or she'd ask, "Daddy, can I lay down with you for a little while?"

And you said, "Of course." And you'd scoot over and that little hot pocket of a burrito would just wedge himself in there.

A long time ago, back in the 1900s, when I was in maybe third or fourth grade, we lived in Dillon, South Carolina, a tiny town. Not much more than a map dot. My daddy and my uncle Phillip tore down an old tobacco barn to reclaim the wood so we could have hardwood floors in our house. The result of that deconstruction meant we had all this wood and tin and stuff in piles in our backyard. Looking at that pile and knowing me and my brother, my dad brought us together and said, "Look here boys, whatever you do, don't go near the lumber. Don't go near the woodpile. Period. There's rusty nails and there's tin, and you can get tetanus. Not to mention snakes and spiders. So, whatever you do, steer clear. Leave it alone."

"Yes, sir."

So what'd I do? The next day, when I woke up, I immediately walked straight to the lumber. It was my dad's fault. He was the one who pointed it out. And like every other kid on planet Earth would have done, I began to rearrange the lumber and tin to build a fort. This was long before Fortnite. There were no screens involved. We had oxygen, dirt, and sun. It was crazy. Your kids should try it.

So, I built this little fort, rearranged some stuff, and in my mind, it was awesome. Had like two little spaces, a place for me to hang out and a living area. I had a little roof on it, windows, and a place to sit. I remember thinking, *Well, if things don't work out in the house, I'll just move out here. This'll be great.*

It was a Saturday, midmorning rolled around, and I was just doing my thing out there. Then I began to get a little sleepy, and anyone that knows me well knows I have the gift of sleep. I mean, I can just…boom. I'm out. It's a spiritual gift, it really is. Clean living. No worries.

As the sun rose higher and it got a little hotter inside that tin hut, I got more and more sleepy and pretty soon, I just stretched out in my new little home. Peace out. He gone. I'm gonzo.

I don't really know how long I was out, but it must have been a pretty good nap because when I awakened my parents are losing their ever-loving minds. I sat up, squinted through the little slit windows, and asked myself, "Wonder what's going on? Why is everybody acting so crazy?" My mom was literally screaming bloody murder. And I couldn't really make out what she was saying until about the third or fourth time. "Joseph Perry Martin III."

That's about the moment it hit me that I might be in trouble. Especially since they were now using my government name. Anytime they go government, it ain't good. So, I thought, *Uh-oh.*

Staring out through the slit, I saw my dad standing beside her, while she aimlessly roamed the neighborhood. Then my dad was out on the back porch screaming at the top of his lungs. And right about here I thought, *Oh, no, I'm a dead man.*

From my little hideaway I could see the street and all my neighbors were walking door-to-door, and everybody had not-real-happy looks on their faces. Remember, this was back in the day when they used to put kids' faces on the backs of milk cartons if they were lost or missing. I'm pretty sure my momma was on the way to Piggly Wiggly with a Polaroid to get my picture on the milk because she thought I'd been stolen. In her defense, I was rather cute. At least that's what she told me.

Knowing that I was about to get whipped like I ain't never been whipped, I began scheming. I looked to the other side of my house, and I saw both police cars from Dillon. Both were parked at my house. This was real bad. My folks had called the po-po. And since both cars were there, that meant the entire police force was now in my yard.

"Yep, I'm a dead man."

My dad's voice was bellowing at this point. "Joby, Joby!" And then he was kind of muttering to himself, "When I catch that boy, I'm going to..."

This was back before my daddy knew Jesus, so I don't want to write that part. I couldn't let him see me in the woodpile of death, so I snuck out of my fort, skirted around our barn, and kind of flanked my dad so he didn't see me from too far away. Then I walked up behind him and innocently tugged on his shirt, at which point he flipped around and I said, "I'm right here."

Astounded, my dad grabbed me by the shoulder and said, "Boy, I don't know whether to whoop you or hug you." Given that it was one of two options, I said, "I'll take a hug."

My dad was not the most affectionate dude. Now, today he's a grandpa so all that's different. When I was a kid, we had to toe the line. My kids? They can get away with anything around him. But in that moment, when he saw me safe and not kidnapped, he melted for a second. He reached out, picked me up, and squeezed me like a father who, when he thought he had lost his son, sent out search parties, called the police, screamed, yelled, called my name, and did whatever it took to find me because I was lost. In that moment, I was all that mattered. But then when I tugged on his shirt, he could celebrate because I was found.

No matter where you come from or what you've done, this is what God the Father does with you when you come to Him. And He does this for all of us. When we bow in surrender to Jesus, we bow as orphans. Rebels. But God the Father, in an act of unmerited mercy, wraps His arms around us and raises us up as sons. And not only as sons, but as heirs. Why? Because only a son can mature into a man. There is no other path.

You and I are not primarily tools in the hand of God to be used or even soldiers in His army to fight; we are primarily sons in God's family to be loved. You should stop and let that sink in. The one singular word that defines you before any other is "son." (And "daughter.") That's just who we are.

PRAY WITH ME

Our good and gracious heavenly Father, God, I love You more than anything because You first loved us. Lord, I thank You that You did not merely come to forgive us but to adopt us into Your family. God, I pray for every man and every woman right now who have a problem with the idea of fatherhood. And God, I thank You that grace abounds when their ideal is unrealized. God, I pray that You would overwhelm them with Your love. And God, we thank You that we can know You as Father, that we are no longer slaves of fear, that we are sons of the most high King, with Jesus as our older brother. God, I pray the truth of that good news would set us free to be free. And God, I pray that if there's anybody who reads these words—any man, any woman, any student right now who doesn't know You as heavenly Father, God—they would surrender their life to You in this very moment and be welcomed into the family of God, adopted into the family of God for the very first time.

God, we pray this in the good, strong name, the only name that matters when you pray, we pray this in the name of Jesus Christ our Lord and Savior. And all God's people said amen.

Amen.

DOING THE STUFF

This is going to stretch some of you, and your family may wonder what's wrong with you, but I want you to act like Jesus and share communion with your family. That's right, gather them around the table. If you're not doing the wine thing right now, use grape juice. Here's why: I know some of you grew up in churches where communion was just one more box you checked before the service was over. This is not that. Not some rote tradition without meaning. Sharing in His body and blood is something Jesus told us to do. To remember. And when we do, we surrender all over and remember his death and His life and the covenant He made with us.

Now, maybe you can spring it on your family and maybe not. You know your family best. So text, call, or, better yet, go old-school and ask them in person, "When can we get together for a family date night?" You may get some pushback, especially if you have teenagers, but that's good. Shows you're pushing in a Godly way. The point is, plan it. Put it on the calendar. And don't let your calendar be the one that pushes this into next month. Do what you have to do, cancel what you have to cancel, to get this done. Tonight would be best. This week is a must. If you push this out, the enemy will slip in and suck your momentum. Don't let him do that. Jesus made a point of doing this. You do the same.

For those of you who need a little help with the wording or you're not sure what to say or how to say it, no problem. I've been speaking a lot of words for a long time, in fact I get paid to do it, so just use mine. Feel free to make them your own. You might read this part to your family:

On the night Jesus was betrayed, he brought together the twelve disciples, and the Bible says that to show them the full extent of

His love, He rose from the table, dressed Himself as a servant, and washed His disciples' feet. After which, He said, *"I have set for you an example. You will be blessed if you do likewise"* (John 13:15).

Dads, stop right there. Jesus just told you and me and all of us to do something, so put this book down, grab a basin, fill it with warm water, and wash your family's feet. I know I said we were serving communion, but this is part of it. Don't skip this. It matters. And don't let your teenagers' rolling eyeballs deter you. They need to see this and be a part of it. It very well may shake some things loose in their hearts.

Family, please don't snicker. Don't walk away. Don't recoil. This matters. A lot. Your husband, your dad, is serving you like Jesus served His disciples. So, be a disciple and let him do it. Jesus really did this with His disciples. Think about that a minute.

Dads, keep reading here: When Jesus had finished, He sat down at the head of the table and shared the Passover meal with His disciples. It's no accident that this is the Passover meal—remember the Passover remembers how blood protected the children of the Israelites from death.

That night at the table, Jesus said, *"Hey, boys, that whole Passover thing, about the blood of the Lamb being on the doorpost of the house and the angel of death passing over, that Lamb is me. I am that Lamb. I am who John the Baptiser said I am when he said, 'Behold, the Lamb of God who's come to take away the sin of the entire world.'"*

After He said this, Jesus held up the bread. Normally, in the Passover meal, He would say rabbi stuff about the Exodus, but not this time. This time, He personalized it and He said, *"This is My body broken for you."* Truth be told, they had no idea what He was talking about until the next day when they were standing at the foot of the cross and they saw the Lamb of God slain for the forgiveness of sin. That was probably when the light bulb went off. Then Jesus said, "*This is my body broken for you. As often as you eat of it, do so in remembrance of Me*" (1 Cor. 11:24).

Dads, say this: "This is Jesus' body broken for you. As often as you eat of it, do this in remembrance of Him." Then break the bread and share it with your family. Family, just receive it.

At the end of the meal, Jesus spoke up again. The disciples had no idea what He was going to say. This time He held up a cup of wine and said, "*This is my blood.*" Now, a lot of people have gotten hung up right here. Is it blood or wine? Tastes like wine to me, but that's not the point. The point is what it represents. He said, "*This is my blood, and this is the cup of a new covenant*" (Matt. 26:28). The old covenant that came from Moses was the covenant of law, and Jesus had fulfilled the law. He had accomplished everything that the law and the prophets said that He would. And so He said, "*The old covenant, it is a covenant of law, but this is the cup of the new covenant, and it's a covenant of grace.*"

Again, they didn't know what He was talking about, but the next day they saw it. On the cross, Jesus drank the full cup of the wrath of God on our behalf. And because of the grace of God, when we partake of the cup of the new covenant in His blood, we can drink of the grace of God for His glory. Jesus said, "*This is my blood shed for you, the cup of the new covenant poured out for the forgiveness and the remission of sins. And as often as you drink of it, you do so in remembrance of me*" (1 Cor. 11:25).

Dads, say this: "This cup is the shed blood of Jesus, the cup of the new covenant poured out for the forgiveness of sins. Drink and do this in remembrance of Him." Family, just drink.

Jesus willingly died in our place on that cross. And in doing so, He became the propitiation for our sin. The body of Jesus Christ became the payment that satisfied then and forever the wrath of God for everyone who would believe. And when He pushed up on

His nail-pierced feet, and said, "Tetelestai," or "It is finished," he adopted every one of us who would believe into the very family of God. Taking communion is bowing before Jesus, and every time we do, He raises us up as sons and daughters of the most high King.

Dads, I don't have a prepared prayer for you to pray. It's your turn. I'm passing the baton. You don't need my words. You've got your own. Family, it'd be a really good thing if you all would gather around this man and let him pray for you and over you. There's something really cool that happens in the kingdom of God when husbands and dads pray over their families.

Dads, I'm crazy proud of and for you and I'm praying for you. Now, just pray.

Ready, break!

FINAL THOUGHTS

Way back in the 1900s, as a college junior, I surrendered to a call to ministry. At the time I was serving in a big old Baptist church where, when you surrender, you got to walk down front. Before God and everybody. It doesn't count if you just do it quietly in your heart. Nothing works back there. You've got to come down front and tell the pastor.

So, as a junior, I did this. Which didn't go over too well with my dad, as I already told you. To make matters more complicated, I had been studying premed. Can you imagine me as your doctor? Yeah, me neither. Anyway, a course change to seminary went over like a lead balloon. I said, "Dad, I'm gonna study to be a preacher." He did not seem impressed. "Why? What do you got to study? You only work a half day a week and only study one book." Today, he sits in the front pew, having surrendered his own life to the Lordship of Jesus. For those of you who have been praying for your one-more's for what seems like an eternity, I prayed for my daddy for thirty-seven years. My point is this: Stay the course. Hold fast. Keep praying. Don't get off your knees. God's not finished with them yet.

Later, that summer, I was serving at a little church outside of Myrtle Beach, South Carolina. I'd run these little Bible studies and we'd have about fifteen kids or something. Once a month we would go to the Pavilion in Myrtle Beach. Anybody ever been to Myrtle Beach? If so, make sure your tetanus shot is up to date. It's a thing, man. Dirty Myrtle. Only really cool thing was we used to watch this band play—couple of local guys. Pretty good, too. First album was called, *Cracked Rear View*. It became the soundtrack for a lot of our lives. Not long after, Hootie and the Blowfish blew up, and where there used to be five hundred people at their shows, now there were five to ten thousand. Anyway, Myrtle Beach was known for the Pavilion. It's like a state fair that never ends. We'd load the kids into the van, drive down there, buy the tickets, and do all the stuff. Baseball toss, haunted mansion, tilt-a-whirl. Off to one side sat Bungee Adventure America.

All the kids were like, "Ooh, let's do it. Let's do it. I want to do it." And I didn't want to do it. Mind you, I'm not a fan of heights. Don't love it. Don't love it at all. But you'd never want to look like a wuss in front of your high school kids if you're a youth pastor. All you youth pastors, jot that down. You've got to be awesome.

So I was like, "Oh, I'd totally do it. I'd do it in a canyon. Off a bridge. Let's go." Well, we got to the counter and turned out, I was the only one old enough to go. And I was like, "Well, sorry guys, don't worry about it." They were like, "No, Pastor, we heard how passionate you were about doing this and we know you want to do it, so we'll wait." All right. So I walked back to the desk and they told me with a smile, "It'll be ninety dollars."

Remember, I was a youth pastor. It was the first and only time in my life I prayed and thanked God for not having enough money to do something. So I walked back to the kids, "Hey kids, I'm out. Ninety bucks. I don't have it, so let's go."

The kids huddled together and after about a minute they said, "Here's ninety bucks."

FINAL THOUGHTS

And I was like, "Dude, I'm a youth pastor. I can't pay you back ninety bucks."

"We don't care. It's our parents' money. Here you go."

Maybe you can see where this is headed.

To begin with, the people who owned the tower of terror weighed you. That's not a fun situation. It's like they're checking to see if you're going to break the bungee. Then you signed this piece of paper that said, "If I die, it's not your fault." And then they marched you into this atomic wedgie suit thing and then stuck you on an elevator so you could be an idiot and jump back down. When I got to the elevator, it was broken. Which was not helping my breathing. You ever seen those people on airplanes breathing into paper bags?

The dude looked at me and says, "It's broken." If there are two words I didn't want to hear in this moment, they are those exact two words. This wasn't good. It's going from bad to horrible.

So I huffed and puffed my way up ten flights of stairs. And my underwear was so far up my crack I thought I'd never get it out. With every step, I was more afraid, more afraid, more afraid, more afraid. If you think one hundred feet looks high from the ground, it's a whole 'nother ball game to stand up there and look down. Seagulls were flying under me. I could see over the tops of tall buildings. I asked Jesus to come into my heart again just in case I'd messed it up somewhere along the way. I was not pumped about this. When I finally I got to the top, to my right stood a seventeen-year-old kid gnawing on a slice of pizza. He sized me up. "'Sup?"

I try to be civil. "Hey, man, I don't know..."

He could care less. "I'm going to hook you up and then I'm going to open this door and you're going to step out."

So I did what I never should have done. I looked. Out into the blackness. Out over planet Earth. Only me and the dry cleaners will ever know the effect of that on me.

Around a mouthful of pizza, he continues, "You want to go head or feet first?"

"Head first." I ain't limping my way into heaven. I was just going to smash my brains all over the concrete while my kids watched. So I leaned out over that thing and saw where some kind person has placed a little air mattress that was supposed to give you something to aim at and make you think the landing would be soft. But, like the elevator, it too was broken. They were not crushing it with the making-me-feel-secure thing. But fear not, the deflated mattress wasn't a problem for them, so they just moved it out of the way, which revealed that some other kind person had spray-painted a target on the cement down there. "Smash brains here."

I had a death grip on the railing, and my flight instructor, who's barely old enough to shave, said, "All right, I'm going to count three, two, one, jump."

I nodded. I'm pretty sure no audible sound came out of my mouth.

So, without really waiting for a thumbs-up from me, he goes, "Three, two, one."

And it's not happening. No can do. I had a white-knuckled death grip on the railing. The Hulk himself could not budge me. Meanwhile, my kids that I'd been loving and preaching the Bible to and caring for and praying for were not loving me back. They were just hurling insults at me.

Evidently, my new friend had seen my kind before, so a second time he said, "Three, two, one."

And still nothing. No power on earth could pry my fingers from that bar.

At this point, my seventeen-year-old friend, who had been sent there by satan to send me to everlasting fire and damnation, looked at me and said: "Dude, just shut up and jump."

Some of the greatest advice I've ever been given in my life came out of the mouth of a seventeen-year-old kid, cramming down a pepperoni pizza atop a bungee tower a hundred feet over Dirty Myrtle.

And it was the very thing I needed to hear. So I stepped off that little platform. Peter Pan'd right out into the stratosphere, where a funny thing happened. Gravity took over and man, it took over fast. I would have screamed like a prepubescent girl watching *The Notebook* or reading a Charles Martin novel, but luckily for me, no sound would come out of my mouth.

Anyway, about the time it started, it was over. I raced to the earth at seven hundred miles an hour, telling Jesus, "I'll see you in a second," aimed my forehead at the bull's-eye, and braced for impact.

Which didn't come, as you can tell, cause I'm sitting here telling you this story. As I careened toward the earth's surface, I felt this slight, then growing, tug on the atomic wedgie suit. The bungee cord extended, the bull's-eye got closer, my spine was stretched five inches, then it stopped getting closer and started getting farther away. This told me I had skipped the pain part completely and was now headed to heaven. I thought I heard angels singing.

Then, gravity took over again and convinced me I was not headed to heaven but was in the process of paying for all of my many sins. So, we did it all over again. Wash, rinse, repeat. When I finally got my feet on the ground, the kids were all laughing at me. To cap it off, the owners of the tower of terror gave me a little T-shirt to commemorate my stupidity. It read, "Shut up and jump." Problem was the only size they had was a medium. If you've ever seen pictures of me or watched me on TV, you know I haven't fit into a medium since I was six. I guess I could've cut the sleeves off and worn it as a halter top, but that never materialized.

The guy said to me, "We came up with this shirt because tough-talking wimps like you show up all the time, pay the money, climb the steps, get to the top, look down, and turn into curdled milk."

Actually, that's not what he said, but I can't write what he said. Anyway, he told me that all of us are alike. We start strong, bragging, then by the top, we're full of excuses as to why we can't go. "Hey man, I'm going to need to walk back down. I got to take these kids home. Their parents trusted me with them. And..." or, "Hey, listen, I'm a pastor and the Bible says, 'Thou shall not bungee jump. And if you push me, you'll go to hell.'" Or, "I'm in my fifties and I pee a little when I do jumping jacks. Can you imagine what'll happen if I vault myself off this thing? I'd pee on everybody."

In Matthew 14, Peter is sitting in the boat during a hurricane-type storm. Jesus is standing out there on the water. Unfazed by the wind and the waves.

Maybe your life is comfortable. Maybe you've been doing the same thing over and over and over and over. Maybe you come to church, you like the songs, you're fairly entertained. Maybe you read this book, checked this box because your wife left it on your nightstand, and you've laughed a few times at my dumb jokes.

But what if? What if right now, Jesus is standing on that water speaking deep in your soul? What if in this moment, despite the storm, He's saying, "Come on, get out of the boat"?

I don't know what "get out of the boat" means for you. It could mean be ridiculously generous. Start that ministry. Share the gospel. Offer forgiveness. Tear up that IOU. Keep the baby. Buy that ring. I can't tell you what it is, but here's what I know, and Mary said it to the servants in Cana—"Do whatever He tells you to do."

I'm not trying to be sacrilegious or put words in God's mouth, but He sent me here to this page, to tell you this—"Dude, shut up and jump."

I implore you by the power of God, just do what it is He has called you to do. And if you are sitting there and that thing is nagging at you and you don't want to do it? You should probably start there.

You want an abundant life? It starts with obedience. And obedience starts with a step. And that step is pretty much guaranteed to take you from comfort to extreme discomfort. But God didn't call you to be comfortable. He called you to be obedient. To trust Him. Put your faith in Him and not in yourself.

Guys, listen to me. Get out of your own head. Stop with the excuses. Stand up. Act like a man. Shut your mouth. And jump.

And when you do, let everything from this moment on be done in love.

PRAY WITH ME

Our good and gracious heavenly Father, Lord, I pray that You through the power of the Holy Spirit would simply give us the faith and the courage to do whatever it is that You've called us to do. God, for some of us, we're scared. Please give us faith when they push us off the platform because we might not have the strength to uncurl our fingers. Lord, we're all scared. We all have excuses. The boat feels safe. But the truth is, we're much safer on the water with You in the midst of a cat 5 than sitting in a sinking boat. Lord, I pray every man, woman, and child reading these pages would just shut up and jump. That they would live a life of extraordinary generosity and give generously. That they'd never quit praying for their one more, that they'd risk the discomfort and share their faith, and that no matter what, they'd do what You are telling them to do. No matter the cost or how scared they might be. Lord, I pray through the power of the Spirit of God, that all of us would shut up and jump. Lord, whatever the thing is that you have called us to do, may we trust You more than we trust the circumstances around us. God, may we know it'll be the greatest jump we ever take in our life because we will jump into the faithful ever-loving hands of our loving, heavenly Father. We pray this in the good, strong name of the only One with arms strong enough to catch us, Jesus. Amen.

FINAL THOUGHTS

DOING THE STUFF

Do I really need to tell you?

For those of you, like me, who are a little thick between the ears or maybe need some help letting go of the railing, let me say this. And yes, I'm speaking directly to you.

Shut up and jump.

ACKNOWLEDGMENTS

I want to thank all of The Church of Eleven22: the elders, staff, and members, for allowing me to do what I do.

ABOUT THE AUTHOR

Joby Martin is the founder and lead pastor of The Church of Eleven22 in Jacksonville, Florida. Since launching the church in 2012, he has led a movement for all people to discover and deepen a relationship with Jesus Christ. In addition to providing The Church of Eleven22 with vision and leadership, Pastor Joby is an author, a national and international preacher, and a teacher. He has been married to his wife, Gretchen, for more than twenty years, and they have a son, JP, and a daughter, Reagan.

Charles Martin is a *New York Times* bestselling author of seventeen novels, including his most recent, *The Record Keeper*. He has also recently authored four nonfiction works, *What If It's True?*, *They Turned the World Upside Down*, *Son of Man*, and *It Is Finished*. His work has been translated into more than thirty-five languages.